The Writing Life

The Writing Life

Ellen Gilchrist

University Press of Mississippi   Jackson

www.upress.state.ms.us

"The Undertaking" on page 35 reprinted courtesy of Louise Glück.

The University Press of Mississippi is a member of the
Association of American University Presses.

FIRST EDITION 2005

∞

Library of Congress Cataloging-in-Publication Data
Gilchrist, Ellen, 1935–
   The writing life / Ellen Gilchrist.—1st ed.
      p. cm.
   ISBN 1-57806-739-1 (cloth : alk. paper)
   1. Gilchrist, Ellen, 1935– 2. Authors, American—20th century—
Biography. 3. Creative writing (Higher education) 4. Authorship.
I. Title.
   PS3557.I34258Z477   2005
813'.54—dc22   2004022120

British Library Cataloging-in-Publication Data available

For Carolyn,
who is a fan of all things beautiful and true
and kind and Zen and hopeful

He is called a writer, not he who writeth in measure only but he who fayneth and formeth a fable and writes things like the truth.

—BEN JOHNSON

CONTENTS

CONTENTS

CONTENTS

PREFACE

This book was inspired by young people. Many of the best essays were dragged out of me by young magazine editors. They would ask me to write about something like balancing life and work or quitting drinking and I would agree and write a superficial piece about the subject. Then the young editor would beg and cajole me to dig deeper and tell more and think harder and I would reluctantly go back to work.

The essays about learning to teach writing were inspired by the two hundred or so students I have had in my care for the last four years. I learned as much from them as I taught them, maybe more. These essays are field notes, as I soldiered on into unknown territory.

The organization of the book is the work of my editor, Craig Gill, who took three hundred pages of manuscript and carved a book from it. I cannot thank him enough for his help.

What else should I say in a preface? Life is short, seize the day, live in the present, commit random acts of kindness and senseless acts of beauty, lighten up, come along, let's take some words for a walk.

Part One: Life

The Middle Way

MAYBE YOU HAVE TO WAIT for happiness. Maybe the rest is only words.

When I was a child I had a book about a small boy in Scotland whose father was a Highlander and whose mother was a Lowlander. All his life they argued in his presence about whether he was a Lowlander or a High-lander and each tried to persuade him of their case.

In the winters they lived with his mother's people and farmed and cared for domestic animals. In the summers they stayed in the Highlands with his father's people and he hunted the high hills with his father and his uncles. He was a strong boy and the altitude caused him to grow powerful lungs. When he called the goats and cattle on his mother's farm his voice rose above the rest. In the hills he sometimes stood and called out across great distances to the other hunters. So he grew until he was almost as tall as a man.

The year he was sixteen, as they were making their way from the Highlands to the Lowlands, they came upon a man sitting on a rock playing bagpipes. The boy had never heard such heavenly music. He begged his parents to let him stay and learn to play bagpipes. Finally, when the man agreed to teach him, his parents left him there. And there he stayed the rest of his life, halfway between the Lowlands and the Highlands, playing beautiful music and looking up and down at the worlds he had left behind. Because his lungs were strong from working on the farm and climbing in the hills he was able to make music so fine it could be heard from miles away.

I loved that story the most of anything I had ever read. I can still see each page of the book in my mind's eye and I think I have finally found a place between the worlds where I can live in peace and do what I was meant to do. The middle way, the Zen masters call it. Ever since I first heard of that I have known that is what I am seeking.

Family and work. Family and work. I can let them be at war, with guilt as their nuclear weapon and mutually assured destruction as their aim, or I can let them nourish each other. In my life, as I have finally arranged it, the loneliness of being a writer and living alone in the Ozark Mountains is balanced against the worry and control issues of being a mother and a grandmother. I move back and forth between these two worlds. Somewhere in the middle I play my bagpipes and am at peace.

Of course, it wasn't always this easy. I have written two books of poetry and eighteen books of fiction about the struggle to free myself from my family and my conditioning so I could write and live as an artist with a mind that was free to roam, discriminate, and choose. I will leave the details of that struggle, which included four marriages, three Caesarean sections, an abortion, twenty-four years of psychotherapy and lots of lovely men, to your imaginations and go on with the story of where I landed, on this holy middle ground which I don't feel the need to fortify or protect, only to be grateful for having, as long as my destiny allows. I tell myself I am satisfied to be here now, but, of course, I would fight to keep my life if I had to, with sharp, number-two lead pencils and legal pads, my weapons of choice for all battles.

Still, I don't remember the events of my life as a struggle. I think of myself as a thinking, planning, terribly energetic competitor in games I believed I could win. It's all perception. If I cried I thought of the tears as some sort of mistake. Later, I learned that tears are unexpressed rage. My father was a professional baseball player until I was born. At our house we had no respect for crybabies. We believed in channel swimmers and home run kings and people who learned to walk after they had polio. My daddy set the bar high. He taught me it didn't matter if you won or lost, it was how you played the game.

Practically speaking I have worked it out this way. Part of the time I live on the Gulf Coast near my family and participate in their lives as hard as I can. I don't change my personality to do that. I am a bossy, highly opinionated person and I say what I think. On the other hand I love them deeply and help them in every way I can. They don't have to ask for help. I see what is needed and I act.

Then, when I have had enough of trying to control the lives of people just as willful and opinionated as I am, I drive back up to the Ozark Mountains and write books and run around with writers, artists, photographers, fitness experts, professors, and politicians. Sometimes I stay away from the coast for months and don't even think about my family unless they call me. If they need me I am here.

Because I don't like to fly on airplanes or stay in hotels I have to make the life I live in Arkansas as rich as I can figure out how to make it. If I have a good life here I can leave my children alone to live their lives without interference. I want to help them but I don't want to need them.

Two years ago I decided I was getting stagnant so I asked the university here to give me a job teaching writing. I had never taught but I thought I would be good at it. I wanted to be with younger people who were not related to me. Also, it was the year my oldest grandson went to college, a rite of passage for both of us. I think subconsciously I wanted to be with other young people who were experiencing what he was. I have always participated very deeply in his life. Perhaps teaching at a university was one more way of staying near him. So, now, to add to my happiness, I am teaching. What I do aside from that is get up at dawn every day and run or walk or work out at the health club. I love endorphins and I love to write and I love to read. I read and read and read. I live like a nun. I eat only fresh vegetables and high protein foods. I drink only water and coffee. I have a group of friends who come over on Sunday afternoons and read the plays of William Shakespeare out loud. We've been doing that for fifteen years. Talk about bagpipes, this is the World Series of intellectual endorphins.

I think I am happy because I have quit trying to find happiness through other people. No one else can give you happiness after you become an adult. Happiness is self-derived and self-created. I derive happiness from the fact that my children and grandchildren are alive and breathing and that I am here to watch their lives unfold. Aside from that it's up to me. "To be alive becomes the fundamental luck each ordinary, compromising day manages to bury," it says on a piece of paper I have tacked up in the room where my children stay when they come to visit. I have internalized that knowledge. I want them to begin to learn it too.

What else? I have learned to wait. I no longer have to *always* be the one who makes things happen. Sometimes

I write every day for months on end. Sometimes I immerse myself in teaching. Sometimes I go to the coast and try to control my progeny's lives. Sometimes I don't do a thing but watch tennis on television and exercise obsessively and read books and go shopping at the mall. I have written and published twenty-two books. I have been the best mother I know how to be and a better grandmother. In the light of that I refuse to feel guilty about a thing, past, present, or forevermore.

Who knows how long my happiness will last? It won't last forever that's for sure, but I have a plan for when it ends. When I can no longer live independently or call the shots about my life or if I become ill with a disease that would make me an invalid, I will hopefully, cheerfully, kill myself. I will find a fast, chemical way to do it and go somewhere where I won't leave a mess and get it over with. Whatever I was will rejoin the dazzling, star-filled carbon mass from which it came. I'll leave my DNA in three sons and twelve grandchildren and that's enough for me. I have told my family for twenty years that is how I intend to die and they all know it's true. No one will be surprised and the ones who loved me will know better than to be sad.

I believe with all my heart and soul that happiness begins with great, good health and is nurtured in solitude. Perhaps the reason so many young mothers are stressed and unhappy is that they never get to be alone long enough to calm down and play the bagpipes. When

I am taking care of small children I can't find time *to take a bath.*

Also, women in my generation had children when they were very young. A nineteen- or twenty-year-old girl is a much different mother than a highly educated, thirty-year-old woman who has had a career and interrupts it to have children. I was a child myself when I had my first two children and I played with them as if I were a child. I'm still pretty childish, which is why small children like to be with me. I lapse back into a childhood state quite easily, as I have a wonderful, inventive mother who taught me to believe that fairies played at night in my sandpile and left footprints on my castles. She would go out at night after I was asleep and walk around the castles with her fingers. Also, she told me that beautiful fairies hid behind the leaves of trees to watch over me. She is ninety-three and still a lovely, ethereal creature.

It may be easier to be a mother when you have never had any real achievements until you produce a baby. Here it is, the reason for existence, and you created it! I think older women probably make better mothers in many ways. But young women are more selfish and you have to be selfish to demand time for yourself when you have children. Young women are closer to the time when they were manipulative and childish and they don't let their babies manipulate them as much as older mothers do. These are only my conclusions from watching children in grocery stores. I love to watch them work on their mothers to get what they want, and, because I am always a child, I'm pulling for them to get the candy and to get it NOW. The other day I watched a little blond beauty pull her mother's face to her and lay her hands on her mother's cheeks and kiss her nose. Needless to say they opened the bag of cookies then and there.

One of the reasons I am happy now is that I did the work I had always dreamed of doing. But I didn't start doing it seriously and professionally until I was forty years old. I have always loved books and always thought of myself as a writer but I didn't have an overwhelming desire to write and publish things until my children were almost grown. I had published things off and on during my life and I enjoyed the process but I had no sustained desire to be a writer. It was just something I knew I could do if I wanted to. I was busy falling in love and getting married to three different men (I married the father of my children twice), and having babies and buying clothes and getting my hair fixed and running in the park and playing tennis. During those years my desire for literature was satisfied by reading. If there was something that needed writing, like the minutes for a PTA meeting or a play for my husband's law firm's dinner party, I wrote it and everyone liked it but I didn't want to keep on writing. To tell the truth I was forty years old before I had enough experience of life to be a writer. I barely knew what I thought, much less what anything meant.

I wouldn't be happy now if I had no progeny. The reason I don't fear death is that every chromosome of me is already in younger people, spread around in all my lovely grandchildren. Some of them have my red hair. Others have my temperament. A few have my verbal skills. One has my cynicism. Several have my vanity and pride.

The years I spent raising my sons are as important to my happiness as the books I have written. If some of that time was frustrating, if occasionally I wondered whether I was wasting my talents, then that was the price I had to pay for being happy now. There are always dues to pay.

The month my first book of fiction was published was also the month my first grandchild was born. "I don't know which thing makes me happier," I told Eudora Welty, in July of that year, just weeks before the two events occurred.

"They aren't in competition, Ellen," she answered.

When I think of that conversation I remember running into her once on the Millsaps College campus, years before, when she was my teacher there. I had my three little redheaded boys with me. They were four and five and two, gorgeous, funny little creatures, fat and powerful, with beautiful faces. I had never mentioned to Eudora that I had children. I suppose it took her by surprise to see me coming down the path with my sons. I think they were wearing white summer outfits. When they were young I loved to dress them in white sailor suits or buttoned-up shirts with ruffles down the front.

"Oh, my," Eudora said. "Are they yours? Do they belong to you?"

"They're mine," I answered. "Aren't they funny?"

"Why would you need anything else?" she said. "Why would you need to be a writer?"

I did not understand what she was saying to me but I do now. Eudora had no children of her own and that year she had lost her father and her brother. Her mother was in a nursing home. Think how my riches must have looked to her. Think how far away from wisdom I was not to know what she was telling me.

In the end happiness is always a balance. I hope the young women of our fortunate world find ways to balance their lives. I hope they learn to rejoice and wait.

OCTOBER 2000

The Shakespeare Group

I HAVE A HUNDRED favorite books. At different times in my life I would have said my favorite book was *Collected Poems* by Edna St. Vincent Millay or Gabriel García Márquez's *One Hundred Years of Solitude* or *Go Down, Moses* by William Faulkner or the collected works of J. D. Salinger or Ernest Hemingway, to name a few.

But if the world as I know it was coming to an end and I had to grab one book to save to help rebuild that world it would be my *Riverside Shakespeare*, although the *Arden Shakespeare* would do, or anything that contained all the plays.

Thirty-eight plays. I would need them all in case a new world happened that contained people who wanted to be writers. They would need to read all thirty-eight to learn that even the greatest writer who ever lived was a novice to begin with, and then got better, and better, and better and better, until he became the best, past, present, and forevermore.

All writers know that Shakespeare was the greatest writer who ever lived. We write in his shadow and most of us are happy to be there. "There are some guys nobody could ever beat, like Mr. Shakespeare," Hemingway wrote, and I knew that quotation and believed it long before I knew why it was true.

I was fifty-two years old before I began to really know the works of William Shakespeare. Now I am sixty-six and I have been reading the plays out loud nearly every Sunday afternoon for fourteen years and I'm beginning to feel I *almost* know these plays. I don't have to worry that this love affair will end. It will take many more years to really sound the magnificence of them. No one could tire of them. They are not only plays. They are great poetry and they contain novels, essays, stand-up comedy routines, satire, metaphor raised to the tenth power.

The political insights are so apt that every Sunday I think I'm reading satires on the latest news from Washington, D.C. "Heavy hangs the head that wears the crown" is a recurrent theme. Newt Gingrich and Bill Clinton would have been solaced by the plays. I keep hoping Laura Bush is reading them to our president now.

Here is what happened that brought Shakespeare into my life so deeply. You could do this too. I am going to tell you how.

In June of 1987 I went over to my friend Margaret Salassi's house to sit on the porch and watch the afternoon turn into evening. She is a graduate of the writing program here and had been with me in poetry workshops when I was there. She is small and pretty and always ready for a challenge.

We were joined by Patti Hayes, whose husband is a writer and another friend of mine.

We were sitting on the swings on a screened-in porch and I said, "I wish we could go to Stratford in England and see some of Shakespeare's plays." I had seen plays there the year before and been dazzled by them although I only half understood what I was seeing. I had studied Shakespeare at Vanderbilt and seen the movies made from the plays. WHAT I HAD NOT DONE WAS READ THEM OUT LOUD, WHICH IS THE ONLY WAY TO KNOW WHAT THEY ARE.

"We could get the plays and read them," Patti said. "We would read them right here in Fayetteville."

"We could read *King Lear*!" I shouted. "Of course we could."

"Let's do it," Margaret said. "Let's do it tonight."

We got on the phone and started calling people and asking them if they wanted to join us. A poet named David Saunders said he would come. So did a beautiful woman named Kathleen who had studied acting when she was a girl.

The head of the writing program laughed when I asked him to come. "You must be crazy," he said. "It takes four and a half hours to read *King Lear*."

"We don't have anything else to do all summer," I answered, and wrote him off as a spoilsport.

At seven that night we met at my house on Mount Sequoyah. We sat around an oblong dining room table and opened our various editions of *King Lear* and began to read. Seven people were there. Most of us could not pronounce all the words, especially the names of the characters, but we were all educated people who loved literature and between us we figured it out, not being afraid to ask for help or stumble bravely on when we made mistakes.

It was a Tuesday night. The next Tuesday we were back at our places at the table reading *Hamlet*. By the second Tuesday we had already begun to have special seats which we keep to this day. Because it was my house I fell into the role of assigning the parts. No one fussed or objected. I would say who would read what and we would press on.

We read on Tuesday nights for several years and then somehow we changed to Sunday afternoons and we have stayed there ever since. We have read every play at least three times. Last year we read them in the order in which they were written.

Reading Shakespeare is a humbling experience for a writer. Here is what could be achieved. Reading them in the order in which they were written is especially inspiring. The early plays aren't very good. They have all the amateur mistakes all writers make. They are derivative and overwritten. But within these plays is the genius that will become *Hamlet* and *Macbeth* and *Henry IV*, parts I and II, and *Romeo and Juliet* and *King Lear* and *The Tempest* and *A Midsummer Night's Dream*.

Just to type the names of the great plays makes me shiver. Every Sunday afternoon when Paul and Henry and Carolyn and Margaret and Patti and Enid and Molly and Kathleen and I gather around my table to begin reading, a hush falls on the room. This is greatness and when we open the books and begin to read we are part of that greatness and partake of it.

If you want an entry into this treasure it would be good to read a book called *Shakespeare: The Invention of the Human*, by Harold Bloom. Or just call up some friends and sit down and open a play and begin to read. It's magic. You will not be sorry that you tried it.

MARCH 2001

How Books Still Change
Our Lives

IT IS SNOWING and it is going to snow. The world in which I live is a wonderland. It is Thursday now. On Sunday night two feet of snow fell on Fayetteville, Arkansas, and changed our lives for a while. I live in a house with glass walls. Outside these windows it is too beautiful to describe in words. Every tree and grass-blade, every rise and valley and fence and wall is part of a white and blue and brown and charcoal geometry. I have a line of Buddhist prayer flags, now covered in ice crystals, barely moving on the branches of a hickory tree. They are the only color except in the late morning when the brave redbirds or yellow-tipped sparrows or ruffled robins come out to search for food.

I live on a small mountain overlooking our town. My house is on the top of that hill. To the northwest and far enough below so that the smoke from their chimney comes in my windows on cloudy days live a young couple that I love. He is an elegant New Yorker who shares my passion for tennis. She is one of the most beautiful women in this town and a second-generation painter. She works in oils and sometimes pastels. Her name is Connie Cramer.

Across the street from my driveway, for this is a cul-de-sac at the end of a one-way street, lives another painter. Her name is Mary Jernigan McCormick. When she was painting full-time she sold her canvases for thousands of dollars as fast as she could paint them. Some of them are normal sized paintings and some are very small, miniature, brilliant, amusing portraits of animals or children or objects. If you see one of the small pieces you want to seize it and carry it around with you and show it to everyone you meet.

Eighteen years ago Mary married a handsome, tall man and gave birth first to William and then to John Tucker McCormick. She continues to paint but it is an occasional thing. Sometimes she has a studio and works as a painter for months, but then she will abandon it and spend huge amounts of time and energy making the costumes and sets for a fifth-grade play or spend an afternoon making a two-by-four-inch bearskin rug for her niece's dollhouse or spend a week building a playhouse out of boxes in the yard and painting the whole thing blue with murals and sewing curtains for the windows and then will let the rain wash it away without a thought.

Sometimes she abandons all these activities and plants a dozen trees in her yard or trains the old-fashioned roses on the fence to climb and grow and have a new life.

The first Christmas she lived across from me she decorated a small pine tree with white lights. It sits on an acre lot with many other taller trees but the lights were only on this one small pine tree. When the sun went down in our neighborhood we would see it and know we were in the hands of an artist.

Even Connie, who is an equally good painter, bows to Mary's genius. We just worship her and that is that.

The night before the snow on Sunday I decided to go out to the bookstore and lay in a supply of toys in case I was housebound. I wasn't looking for anything special. I was just poking around the bookstore. On the bargain rack I found a book of paintings called *Impressionists in Winter: Effets de Neige*. On the cover was a detail from a painting I had seen five years before at a show in San Francisco and been thinking about ever since. The painting is by Alfred Sisley and is called *Snow at Louveciennes*. The book was a bound catalog from the show. I took it to a table and began to pore over the plates. Dozens of dazzling impressionist paintings of snow. I couldn't believe my luck. In case it snowed I would be ready. I went back to the bargain table. There were two more copies of the book. One had a tear on the cover so I left it but I bought the second copy to take to Connie because she has been painting lately and I knew she would love it also. I can lend mine to Mary, I decided. I don't want to buy three of them to have in one small cul-de-sac neighborhood. That would be excessive.

I drove home and ran to Connie's house to give her the book. That night it snowed. The snow was so soft it did not wake me up when it was falling. I woke and opened the drapes and there it was, an impressionist painting made of our yards and swings and trees and walls and skies, all in my favorite colors, white and blue and charcoal black.

As soon as I thought she was awake I called Mary and told her I had something she had to see. "This is important," I said. "I know the children are out of school but you have to come over."

"As soon as I can, I will," she answered.

At four that afternoon she finally made it across the street. I made ginger tea and watched her open the book. I had been having a lovely time all day working on a novel and sitting at the table looking out the windows at the snow and looking at the paintings of the snow and wishing I knew how to paint. Because of the paintings I knew to watch for shadows in the snow and notice how the smallest bird can draw the eye to form a tableau.

I was playing a CD of Radu Lupu and the Israeli Philharmonic Orchestra playing Beethoven's Piano Concertos nos. 1 and 2. I stood by a window and watched Mary looking at the Monets and Sisleys and Renoirs and Pissarros and Caillebottes and Gaugins. It is a world to which she belongs. She is a full-fledged and lifetime member, as is my neighbor, Connie Cramer, who had simply opened her book, stretched a canvas and started painting.

I asked Mary to take the book home with her. I knew it would not be good for her to leave it now that she had started looking at it. It would be like someone taking a book of poems from me when I had not finished reading it.

The snow let up the next afternoon and I drove down the icy hill and back out to the mall and bought the third copy of *Impressionists in Winter*. I had been a fool to leave it there that long. I had taken a terrible chance, for there are many writers and painters in Fayetteville, Arkansas, and plenty of them are crazy enough to drive in snow.

I came home and carried the third copy to Mary's house and handed it to her. "I stretched a small canvas about an hour ago," she said. "Thank you so much for getting this for me."

"Thanks for living next to me," I said.

I didn't bother to thank her again for shoveling off the path to my house, which she and her sons had done the day before without telling me they were doing it. Stopping painting to bring William and John Tucker into the world was exactly the sort of thing you would expect a really creative person to know to do.

Not only because William and John Tucker are young and beautiful and we love watching them grow into men but because they can shovel snow and play in the blue playhouse when you build it and in general make the world worth saving and keeping safe.

I am the luckiest woman in the world to have artists live around me. I am the luckiest woman who ever had two feet of snow fall on her house, after having had the luck to go out to a bookstore the night before it happened. Hooray.

FEBRUARY 2003

Casting My Lot with the Gypsies

THIS IS A STORY about growing up, about learning and becoming influenced. I am telling it in deep retrospect, many years after I began to trust my own ideas and not those of other people. A series of powerful, charismatic people influenced me as I grew to be the person I am now, but none more powerfully and strangely than Jane Reid Petty, the founder, director, and principal lead actress of New Stage Theatre in Jackson, Mississippi. Jane is dead now and I miss her. She was the ultimate actress, always on, always posed, always in scene. When I had been with her I played her, sometimes for hours.

She introduced me to psychotherapy. She was the first person I ever knew who went to a psychotherapist and lay down upon a couch and came to understand how our childhoods influence our later lives.

She also introduced me to the theatre. There is nothing on earth as much fun as putting on a play. Most art is done by solitary people alone in their lairs. In the theatre people get together to create, to fight and compromise and bargain and plot and sometimes triumph.

Fortunately I had no desire to act so Jane and I were never in competition in her main arena. She wanted to be a writer also but she wasn't good at it so she let me have that and used my skills to further her own ideas. She would have made a wonderful corporate executive. She knew how to use other people's talents to achieve mutual goals and she always gave praise and honor where it was due.

She talked Eudora Welty into allowing the two of us to turn Eudora's stories into a play and produce it at New Stage. It was a great success. Later the new public television station filmed it and it won a national award for script writing. We were listed as coauthors, although I actually did the writing and the words were mostly Eudora Welty's. It was called *A Season of Green,* a phrase of Eudora's that had already been used as the title of a book of criticism. I always thought of the play as Eudora's work and was glad to let Jane share in the writing credits. I had work of my own to do and was busy getting married for the fourth time so I didn't care who got credit for what.

It was spring when Eudora agreed to the project and Jane and I took copies of all her books and drove down to the Mississippi coast and stayed in a house at Pass Christian and wrote the play. I would type all day while Jane read and shopped for groceries. By the end of seven days we had a manuscript. We took it back to

Jackson and had a meeting in Jane's living room. Frank Haines, the theatre critic of the *Jackson Daily News*, was slated to direct the play. He went crazy when he saw what I had written. "It's too long," he screamed. "My God, it's four times too long."

Frank took the manuscript home and cut it and shaped it and we had another meeting and read what he had done and then I basically lost interest since I liked it the way that I had done it.

The night the play opened was exciting. I had a short, pink, formal dress and silver high-heeled sandals and my new boyfriend came up to Jackson from New Orleans and was duly impressed. Later, after I had married him, I came to Jackson alone to watch the filming for the television production. I sat in a sound booth with Eudora and she kept saying the play was mine and Jane's when of course it wasn't since most of the words were hers.

Here then is a short history of how I went from being a bored housewife to a playwright in two short years.

Don't try this at home unless you're ready to put a strain on your normal relationships. Joining New Stage Theatre was synonymous with getting a divorce. Adultery, divorce, smoking, drinking, egomania, selfishness, there was nothing on Broadway that we didn't have right there in Jackson, Mississippi. We even had a New York director and, of course, he was gay. We had gay men and lesbians but since I was neither I never noticed that any of them were gay. Actually I only sort of half believed they were gay when they told me that they were.

"IT'S EPHEMERAL, MY DEAR. THAT'S THE GLORY OF IT." I was twenty-six years old and I had just come home to Jackson, Mississippi, to live among my family and have my mother's maids take care of my children. I had never meant to be married and have children anyway. I had meant to go off to New York City and be a writer but nature had caught me off guard and for six years I had been struggling good-naturedly to cook and clean and nurse babies. I liked the babies. I thought they were adorable. I would have killed or died for them but I didn't like my husband very much. He was too sober, too serious, too left-brained. Anyway, I had struggled as valiantly as possible and now I had a second chance. My husband had agreed to come work for my father and we had a new house in a good neighborhood with a maid coming in every day and enough money to stretch out and rejoin a larger world.

I began by going back to college. I was admitted into an exclusive writing class being taught by Eudora Welty. It was there that I met the THEATRE PEOPLE. I adored them from the moment I met them. I threw myself into their world. I got money from my daddy and gave it to them for their project, which was starting a theatre in an old church in a black neighborhood and having integrated audiences watch plays Little Theatre wouldn't let them do.

This was 1966. A new day was dawning in parts of Jackson, Mississippi, and I had come home just in time to get in on the party. It was exciting. And it was dangerous, which made it more exciting to me. I had a strong husband and a rich daddy and two big brothers. I had nothing to fear. As long as the maids kept showing up so I didn't miss any of the rehearsals of the plays.

New words started creeping into my vocabulary. Albee, Pinter, Uta Hagen, lesbian, ménage à trois. The backstage dramas that accompanied the founding of New Stage Theatre of Jackson, Mississippi, far outdid anything being mounted on the circular stage that now took the place of the altar.

The psychiatrists in Jackson were mad about the theatre. They would come on Wednesday nights and sit with their feet up on the stage. They would laugh out loud at the subtlest jokes and then, on Mondays and Tuesdays, they would listen to their patients among the actors tell them stories about the cast parties. We had cast parties nearly every week and large ones at the end of our two-week runs.

I can barely remember the parties. All I can remember for sure is a black satin evening suit with a white satin vest I ordered after I saw it on the cover of *Vogue*. And crystal glasses filled with cold, sweet, Beefeater gin and new worlds opening up around me like the petals of cape jasmine or magnolia.

We had lured a great director from New York City to come and live among us. He had spent several years at the Alley Theatre in Houston, Texas, and he was vibrant and exciting and at the height of his powers. I was too shy to act in the plays. I collected props and costume jewelry and gave New Stage all the money I could get from my father and adulation without end. The director was charmed by me, probably because I didn't want any roles. He offered one time to let me be the corpse who is taken from the set in the first scene but I declined. He had said I must promise to stay sober for every rehearsal and two weeks of performance and I didn't think it was worth that, even though the corpse did get to wear a stunning nurse's uniform from the 1920s.

Needless to say my marriage was falling apart. It was falling apart before I met the theatre people but now the process was accelerated. My husband refused to go to parties with people whose vocabularies included lesbian and gay so we looked at our failing marriage and decided to let it fail. He got into the station wagon my father had given us and drove home to Georgia to find a life he wanted to live. I called my brother and he brought me a new car and I got into it and drove down to the theatre to see what was going on.

Jane Petty was the guiding light of New Stage. She had studied with Uta Hagen. She had lured the director to Jackson. She kept the rest of us inspired. She was a great actress.

She was also, hands down, the single most powerful person I have ever known in my life. She had been *in psychotherapy*. She said critical things about *her own mother* and *the family* in general and she laughed when she said these things and then would raise her eyebrows and look at me and ask, don't you think so? She laughed a lot when she said shocking things and used the plays we were producing to illustrate what she meant by traps and pitfalls and scapegoats and Procrustean beds.

I loved her. I threw myself at her feet. I ran errands for her. I learned from her. She never laughed at my ignorance of things she took for granted. She taught me about the theatre and in return I gave her books of poetry to read, as that was the art I knew most about.

Luckily for me I was taking a course in Greek drama at this time or I would not have been able to understand much of what Jane was teaching me: that theatre is religion, that its roots spring from the sacred, which is why we must dress up for performances and make everything as perfect as we can and present our plays, even the comedies, in "the holy hush of sacrifice."

It was easy for me to believe that theatre was religion because I thought poetry was the bread of life and the plays we were doing were poetry. I was reading Aristotle and I believed him when he said that art must break open and release the audience, must change the audience and challenge them. I was twenty-six years old. I wanted to be challenged and changed and taught.

Years later when I became friends with a woman who had been the producer of *Playhouse 90*, which produced the first great television dramas, she said to me that when she graduated from Vassar she had thought she would get married and raise children. "Then I changed my mind," she added. "I met Buckminster Fuller and Isamu Noguchi and went to Europe with them. I cast my lot with the gypsies."

That is what I was doing when I drove every night down to the black neighborhood where we were rehearsing plays and photographing actors and hammering and nailing and painting walls and sets and recushioning pews and screwing lights into the ceiling. These people had so much energy they could have done anything. Also, they had imaginations which were as wild as my own.

Ivan Rider—that was the director's name—began to cast black people in the plays. We invited black people to the performances. Jane had dinner parties for visiting black professors at Tougaloo College. I was dazzled and scared.

I was living with my parents on their estate outside of Jackson in Rankin County. On a neighboring farm the Ku Klux Klan had meetings and built fires. Driving home from New Stage Theatre to my parents' home was like going from one century to another. I was scared of what we were doing at New Stage but I would not have stopped doing it for anything in the world. It was the most exciting thing I had ever known. I was being challenged and changed and broken open and filled with new ideas. The idea of justice became very important to me. I was majoring in philosophy at Millsaps College, where I had enrolled full-time after taking Eudora's class there. Only philosophy and history and poetry could save me now.

I began to publish the poetry I was writing. I was being fed great literature at the college and I was being fed language at its most intense as I sat in the pews and listened to rehearsals of *Tiny Alice* and *Everything in the Garden* and *The Skin of Our Teeth*. Sometimes I think I learned to write comedy from watching twenty or thirty rehearsals and performances of *The Skin of Our Teeth*. No wonder my poetry was getting good enough to be published. I was listening to language that insisted on irony and metaphor and truth.

Several times crosses were burned in front of our theatre. They were also being burned in the front yards of some of our patrons. A woman named Patricia Derian took her cross inside her house and built a pond around it. I don't know what happened to the crosses that were burned at our church. I half understood what was happening and the other half was in denial. I have been completely sober for more than thirty years. I wish everyone was completely sober from the cradle to the grave. Still, I know that gin and wine were part of what was happening to me in those years. I don't think I would have driven so gaily down to that black neighborhood if I hadn't been half tight most afternoons after six o'clock. Perhaps I would have been brave enough cold sober but I doubt it. I was sober when I marched in the civil rights protests, when the theatre people told me that was where they were going and I went along. I was scared to death and sober.

I was sober on the day we woke to the news that the rabbi's house and library had been bombed. I spent the morning walking among the rubble that had been his great-grandfather's books. Perhaps the excitement and charged wisdom and notion of justice and the examples I was being set would have been enough without the gin. I would like to think so but as I said, I doubt it.

It is fortunate that I was twenty-six and twenty-seven and twenty-eight years old when all this was taking place. It took a lot of energy to have three children and college classes and New Stage Theatre and poetry and philosophy and also drink gin. Even though I had the maids to take care of the children I am dazzled when I look back on those years and think of what was happening to me.

The culture was being broken open and changed and I was one of the lucky people who got taken along for the ride. I am glad my epiphanies and catharses took place in the darkened mystery of a theatre. I watched almost every rehearsal of every play and would weep when the performances were over. Ephemeral, that was another word I learned. "Plays have to end," Jane taught me. "Theatre is ephemeral. That is part of the wonder and greatness of it. Every performance is unique. If you miss that moment it is gone forever. If you were lucky to be there it lives in your memory. When everyone who saw a performance dies then it is over for good."

"But why can't we film it," I would answer, as this was before the advent of personal video cameras. "Bring in some movie cameras. I can't bear for this play to be over. I can't stand it when they strike the sets and it is done."

Now, so many years later, I'm glad there were no video cameras to record Ivan's production of *The Skin of Our Teeth*. My memory of the first performance of that play, of the moment the lights went down and the gels came on and the narrator began to tell us where we were and what was happening, is as clear and as pure as the moment it happened. I wouldn't want it to be clouded by anything as ephemeral as reality or a film.

The years I spent in Jackson as part of New Stage Theatre were not my final escape from the bourgeoisie but they were the beginning. A wedge had been made into my soul and into the system of belief that had trapped me like Caliban in a tree. I had met people with imagination who acted on what they thought was true and just. Later I would read a poem by Louise Glück that said much of what I felt in those years. It is called "The Undertaking" and this is part of it.

The darkness lifts, imagine, in your lifetime.
. . . .
          : the light
looks after you, you feel the waves' goodwill
as arms widen over water; Love,

the key is turned. Extend yourself—
it is the Nile, the sun is shining,
everywhere you turn is luck.

The Consolations of Art

IN 1997 I AGREED to be part of a literacy fund-raiser sponsored by the *New Yorker*. I agreed to write a letter to whoever purchased me. My subject was "The consolations of Art." A woman named Ellen Geneo purchased me. Here is the letter that I wrote to her.

Dear Ellen Geneo,
I have been thinking about this letter for some months now as my eighty-eight-year-old father died in the fall and I have had need of the concept as well as the reality. During the month when he was on his deathbed I spent all my spare time in bookstores. Since I was a child I have not spent that much time in a bookstore or library. I was there nearly every day for at least an hour. I was buying five or six books at a time to give to people for Christmas presents and then I was going back and buying copies of the same books for myself. I built a fort of books against myself and my father's death. Some of the books were actually helpful in finding my way through the maze of denial and emotions I was experiencing. *The Tibetan Book of Living and Dying; God, A Biography;*

An Atlas of Human Anatomy; *Everyday Zen*; *The Collected Poems of Robert Frost*, with the haunting and brilliant poem "Provide, Provide," which was the main poem that kept occurring to me during those weeks.

So when I say the consolations of art I mostly mean, for me, the consolations of written books. The heft, the feel, the touch, the mighty consolation they have always been to me in every way. Music, especially Bach, and, this year, Bach played by Christopher Parkening on a classical guitar or the beautiful flute music of Paula Robson, which came in the mail as a gift from the artist on the worst of the days that led to the end of my having a father, have also been an unmeasurable consolation. Music coming down to us through the centuries. From Johann Sebastian Bach and Ludwig van Beethoven and all the thousands who have followed and played them and the makers of violins and pianos and flutes and the patrons like you who have inspired every artist who ever lived have come the vast exaltations which make us glad to live in the midst of contradictions.

So I thank you for wanting this letter. Even before you knew you wanted it or I knew who it would be for I was profiting from the thought that it might be wanted. I had this letter and you on my mind as I surrounded myself with music and books in a small house on the coast that is papered with posters from museums and thought that Van Gogh and Vermeer and Botticelli and Leonardo da Vinci and Cézanne and

Monet were already at the place to which my father now was traveling.

I never loved painting and music and literature and philosophy as I loved them this year because I had never really needed them before. All my love had been to prepare me to throw myself into their charms when my need became great.

I hope that your life is filled with these great expressions of man's hope and glory and praise. For today and every day and so that when you need them they will be there.

Thrive, flourish, "Dance in the fullness of time."
Ellen Gilchrist

Postscript

There was one other thing I meant to tell you. After the funeral I flew to Atlanta to the press screening of the four-hour version of *Hamlet* directed by Kenneth Branagh. I flew all that way to heal myself, and to hear, writ large on the big screen, that the "common theme is the death of fathers." I thought of you and this letter as I was traveling and so could not leave it out as I write.

FEBRUARY 1997

The Only Constant Is Change, and Yet, I Still Won't Use a Computer

I LEARNED TO TYPE when I was twelve years old. When I finished the class my father bought me a Royal portable typewriter with a typewriter table and I set the thing up in the middle of my bedroom and started typing. The next week I redecorated my bedroom to match the typewriter. Down came the beautiful hand-hemmed white lace curtains and off went the beautiful flowered bedspread and dressing table skirt. Down came the reproductions of Gainsborough and William Blake's illustrations for *Pilgrim's Progress*. Up went black and yellow striped awning and a severe white bedspread.

I had become a writer by the simple act of owning a typewriter and now I was ready to write in earnest. I wrote poetry on the typewriter. I wrote journals and diary entries by hand in leatherbound accounting books I bought at the dime store.

When I finished a poem I would take it out of the typewriter and edit it by hand with a number-two lead pencil and then retype it with the changes. I kept every draft of every poem in a letter-sized cardboard box. I kept the accounting books in a drawer of a table by my bed. My parents would never have dreamed of coming into my room and reading what I was writing so I would take my writing down to where my parents were and read it to them out loud. In the late afternoons they would be in the living room or out on the porch if it was warm. Neighbors and friends would stop by and have a drink of my father's expensive scotch whiskey and they would talk and gossip. One afternoon a woman my mother's age was there. Her name was Betty Milliken and she was an editor at the local newspaper. She liked the poems I showed her and asked me if I would like to write a column for her newspaper and maybe end it with a poem. She was a great fan of Dorothy Parker and liked the short silly poems I was writing. The next week she gave me a collection of Dorothy Parker's poetry and I went down to the newspaper office and sat down at a typewriter and wrote a thousand-word essay about something that was going on in the small town of Franklin, Kentucky, and ended it with a poem on the subject of the essay.

I was a sophomore in high school, either fourteen or fifteen years old. They hired me on the spot. I was paid five dollars a week to get out of school on Wednesday afternoons and come to the newspaper and write a column. While I was at the office I also emptied the ashtrays and fed Betty's small white dog. Both Betty and the male editor were chain smokers so I bought some cigarettes and began to smoke with them. I had tried it several times in the past but it made me sick. Now I smoked happily away and learned all about the teletype machine and how print is set and I met deadlines and had bylines and my photograph in the paper and got my paycheck and spent it on doughnuts and hair curlers and books when I could get to the bookstore in Nashville. There was no bookstore in Franklin and the public library wasn't very good so I depended on books I borrowed from people. At school I was taking Latin and translating Caesar's *Gallic Wars*. At home I was a poet. On Wednesday afternoons I was a columnist for a newspaper.

A man in Nashville began to read my newspaper columns on the radio every Thursday morning.

All of this has a great deal to do with why I won't learn how to use a computer. I have had a lot of happiness and luck with my own system of writing and editing by hand and on a typewriter. A screen and the Internet would come between me and my muse. I like it just as it is. I write first drafts on the typewriter and then I edit them by hand. I save every draft in letter-size cardboard boxes. So far I have almost never had to go back and look at old drafts except when I was writing my first novel but you never can tell. At any moment I may want to revisit the moment when I excised a dangling participle or changed the name of a character so I wouldn't get sued. I like computers and because of them the papers my students hand in to me have fewer spelling errors and better margins. I am fascinated by the technology that makes computers work but I am not able to wait thirty seconds for a piece of machinery to catch up with my imagination. I don't stand in lines and I don't wait on computers. I sit down with a legal pad and some number-two lead pencils or I go to my typewriter and I type. If the typewriter breaks I pull the spare one out of the closet and use that. If the electricity goes off I go back to the legal pads.

I haven't written any poetry in a long time but I read it and I miss it. It is so hard to write. So hard to finish, so hard to find the exact word to make it shine. In honor of my youth I will write a poem to finish this essay. It is spring in the Ozark Mountains. The yellow flowers are blooming and the birds wake me at dawn and last night five planets lined up by the moon in the western sky. If that doesn't inspire me to poetry what will?

Not to mention that my first great-grandchild is happily growing inside the womb of a beautiful college soccer player and art major named Courtney Hall Walker. My luck is running strong this year and I am grateful for it.

APRIL 2001

How I Got Stronger and Smarter Instead of Stupider and Sadder

AS I APPROACHED THE AGE OF FORTY, four things happened that changed my life dramatically. I went into psychotherapy, I stopped drinking, I ran a marathon, and I started writing again for the first time in seven years.

Of these four things the most important was that I stopped drinking. Without that the other three might not have been possible.

You can't understand how I quit drinking unless you understand how I became a drunk. I never meant to drink too much. I meant to be a beautiful woman raising a glass of wine to my lover, then dancing the night away in a Balenciaga gown. I meant to look like Lauren Bacall and Hemingway's heroines and talk like Dorothy Parker and Edna St. Vincent Millay. I didn't know they were alcoholics any more than later on I knew that I was one. I had not been educated to see the warning signs nor did I feel free to ask for information when I began to think I had a problem.

I lived in a world where alcohol was served at every meeting and function and anyone over sixteen was allowed, even expected, to drink.

I always got drunk if I had anything to drink. From the first whiskey I was given, on a New Year's Eve by the junior high school basketball coach, to the last terrible night when I fell down a flight of stairs and had a brain concussion, if I drank alcohol I ended up drunk.

During those twenty-four years I tried to quit but I didn't know how because I didn't understand what was wrong with me and my guilt over my behavior was so severe I couldn't bear to face what little information I had.

I remember seeing an article in a woman's magazine called "How to Tell if You Are an Alcoholic." The article was advertised on the cover and I bought the magazine and ran home to read the article. It was a test. There were ten questions and if you answered yes to more than six you were an alcoholic. I think I answered yes to most of them. I hid the magazine but I couldn't stop thinking about the questions.

I was two people when I was a drunk. On the outside I was energetic, bright, optimistic, attractive. On the inside I didn't know what was wrong with me. I couldn't understand why everything I did turned to dust, why my marriages didn't last, why I couldn't achieve my goals, why years were going by and my talents were being wasted. My grandfather said he would rather a child of his be dead than be a drunk. Many times I wanted to be dead during the years when I was a drunk. I could not understand why it kept happening. Why time after time I would set out to have two drinks and end up sleeping God knows where, having lost my car keys, my shoes, my sanity, my health.

My strong constitution and good immune system were my enemies during those years. So was Dexedrine after a physician prescribed it for me during a pregnancy, a common practice during the 1950s. It became harder and harder to obtain as the years went by but I could occasionally get a physician to give me a prescription for a few of them. If I had a hangover I could take two aspirins and a Dexedrine and be as good as new by afternoon.

I did not know what was wrong with me. I did not know that I was an alcoholic. I did not know that what I was doing confused and harmed my children and set them a terrible example.

I thought it was lack of WILL POWER that made me get drunk. I thought it was a CHARACTER FLAW. I knew nothing about blood sugar or insulin or how alcohol makes a person drunk. I didn't know what alcohol is. It is highly concentrated sugar. Like all sugar it is highly addictive. Alcohol destroys the brain's ability to have pleasure in other things. It is like swallowing razor blades. It is like battery acid. It turns into formaldehyde and formic acid in the brain. Formic acid is the stuff of bee stings.

Finally, when I was in my late thirties, I was saved from my addiction. I was saved by knowledge and information and by the help of two great psychiatrists, a behaviorist and a psychotherapist.

It was the turning point in my life. I was living in New Orleans at the time, across the street from Tulane University. On the morning that the good, sober, happy part of my life began I was out running on the Tulane track with my best friend. It was a lovely spring morning, cool for New Orleans, and perfect for running, but I was in a bad mood and feeling guilty. The night before I had barged into my friend's house while she was having a date with a gorgeous French rugby player. I had been drunk when I arrived and after I got there I got drunker.

I don't know why she even came out to the track to meet me the next morning but she did. After we had run about three laps she brought it up. "I don't want you to come over anymore when you're drinking," she said.

"I know," I answered. "I'm so sorry. I don't know why I did it."

"Maybe you need to see a psychiatrist," she suggested. "Diana is seeing one who got her to stop." Diana was a beautiful friend who had been queen of Mardi Gras. Queen of Rex. A very big deal in New Orleans.

"Maybe I will," I answered. "What's his name?"

"His name is Chet Scrignar," she answered. "He's a behaviorist. Diana's crazy about him. She says he's really helped her."

I went home from the track and looked up the phone number and called it. I had not let the thought of a psychiatrist enter my mind since an experience I had five years before. A doctor in Jackson, Mississippi, had given me Antabuse without explaining clearly its dangers. I drank while taking it and almost died from the reaction. But the incident at my friend's house with the French rugby player was really bad. It was the last straw in a series of drunken embarrassments. I had to do something and I knew it.

Dr. Scrignar answered the phone himself. He was very nice and I felt better just making an appointment with him. I may even have told him about my prior experience with Antabuse. Anyway, I made an appointment for the next afternoon.

Dr. Scrignar was a behaviorist who had once been a psychotherapist but had quit because he couldn't stand the slowness of the "talking cure." He had been a track star at a midwestern college and gone to medical school to become a surgeon. When he lost his sight due to a detached retina he went into psychotherapy but it was not a good fit for his personality so he switched to behaviorism.

He was great with addictions. He attacked the problem of my drinking with every tool in his kit. He put me on Antabuse, he hypnotized me, he bribed me with occasional small prescriptions for Dexedrine, he begged me, he charmed me, he took me for walks on cobblestones to show me how he had overcome his blindness, he marched me down to the Tulane University School of Medicine and made me look at slides of diseased livers. Most of all he taught me that alcoholism is a disease. He taught me about blood sugar and insulin and why I couldn't stop once I started drinking.

Every culture has made intoxicating drinks and developed complicated and sometimes beautiful rituals for imbibing them. Every culture has had its victims of these rituals.

I am one of those victims because I am hypersensitive to sugar. When I eat sugar in any form, before we even get to the highly concentrated sugar that is alcohol, my blood sugar levels rise dramatically and insulin has to rush in and get rid of the sugar. My insulin is so good at this that it gets rid of all the sugar in my blood and I am savagely hungry for more of the source of the sugar. Plus all the craziness that goes on in my brain when I drink. A few times since I quit drinking I have tried to have one glass of wine to see if I can. I can usually have one glass of wine that night but within the next few days I will try it again and that time I will get drunk. This scares me absolutely to death and I either take Antabuse for a week or two or sit in zazen for hours or go back into psychotherapy.

The effect that alcohol has on me is dramatic. Perhaps I am the canary in the coal mine. But all alcoholics share the sugar sensitive tendency that I have described. If you have ever gotten drunk when you didn't want to you are an alcoholic and you need to seek counseling and learn about the chemistry of addiction.

There is a rush of pleasure when the effects of alcohol first reach the brain, a silly dizzying pleasure as the higher reasoning powers let go and the superego disappears. I love that feeling and I have found a lot of ways to reproduce it in a sober life. You don't get the instantaneous rush of joy but you don't end up with a hangover, depression, and guilt either.

Once when I was drinking I went down to Ochsner's Clinic and had a terrible six-hour operation to undo a tubal ligation because I had told my husband that the reason I drank was that I wanted to have a child for him. After I said it I had to prove it by having this terrible, unsuccessful surgery.

Once I went down to the French Quarter in New Orleans and tried to get the whores in a whorehouse to come home and live in our house and stop being whores.

I should make a list of things I did when I was drinking that no one would believe anyone would do, much less a nice girl from a nice family who had been educated in good schools and raised by sober parents.

The things you don't know can kill you. I can write this because I know I am a well-meaning person. I was

49

doing the best I could given the information I had at the time. Thank God my best friend was strong enough to tell me I had to quit. Thank God I listened to her.

It was spring when I began to work with Dr. Scrignar. I had to learn many things and unlearn many others. At first I kept on going to the endless round of parties that are the life of uptown New Orleans society. Finally I stopped going to the parties. I was finding other things to do. I began running six miles every morning in Audubon Park, I played tennis, I sat in zazen, I practiced yoga. I read and read and read. I began to write seriously for the first time in seven years.

I was waking up. I was freeing myself from the burden of guilt that people who drink too much carry with them all the time.

I kept on working with Chet Scrignar for several years. After that I went into psychotherapy with a Freudian who helped me understand the psychological causes of my addiction. This work freed me to become a real writer, with the strength to face the truth and to write freely and truly about the world I saw around me.

I am one of the lucky ones. I got help and I got well. "Thank God for Chet Scrignar and what he did for you," my Freudian said to me many times. Amen to that.

SEPTEMBER 2002

Part Two: Writing

How I Wrote a Book of Short Stories in Three Months

I WROTE MOST OF THEM in three months. I wrote the first two stories laboriously over a period of six or seven months.

The book is called *In the Land of Dreamy Dreams*. It is one hundred and sixty-seven pages long. It has been published three times and is still in print. It has sold six or seven hundred thousand copies and is the bedrock of my reputation as a short-story writer.

The opening lines of the book are: "Tom and Letty Wilson were rich in everything. They were rich in friends because Tom was a vice-president of the Whitney Bank of New Orleans and liked doing business with his friends, and because Letty was vice-president of the Junior League of New Orleans and had her picture in the paper every year at the Symphony ball.

"The Wilsons were rich in knowing exactly who they were because every year from Epiphany to Fat Tuesday they flew the beautiful green and gold and purple flag outside their house that meant that Letty had been queen of Mardi Gras the year she was a debutante. Not that Letty was foolish enough to take the flag seriously . . ."

The book ends with these lines: "Later, the ladies went into the house to make a cold supper for anyone who felt like eating and Matille walked down to the bayou and stood for a long time staring down into the water, feeling strangely elated, as though this were some marvelous joke Shelby had dreamed up.

"She stared down into the tree roots, deep down into the muddy water, down to the place where Shelby's pearl waited, grew and moved inside the soft, watery flesh of its mother, luminous and perfect and alive, as cold as the moon in the winter sky."

In between those two quotations are one hundred and sixty-seven pages of the best writing I have ever done, before or since. The muse was with me all the time while I wrote *In the Land of Dreamy Dreams*. I had been writing poetry, seriously and constantly, for six years. I had published a lot of it and I had learned how to polish and edit poetry until it shone like a mirror. Now I turned those skills to the task of writing short fiction.

A teacher at the university where I now teach taught me how to write a short story. I took his class for two months while I wrote the first story in *In the Land of Dreamy Dreams*. Then I went home to New Orleans and wrote the rest of the book. I wrote it in a fever. Writing short fiction seemed "as easy as walking down a tree-lined street" compared to writing poetry. All my poetic skills were still very sharp, I suppose, but it was more than that. I was in one of the spells that artists all know can happen. I knew what I wanted to write about and I just sat down and wrote it.

As I finished the stories I would mail them one by one to Bill Harrison, the teacher who had helped me, and he generously read them and made suggestions. Sometime in the fall he called and told me he wanted to send the book to his agent, but I said, no, I didn't want any strangers in New York City judging my work. "Then let me give it to Miller Williams," he suggested. "He is the editor of the new University of Arkansas Press. He's looking for a book of fiction to be the lead piece for the press."

"All right," I said. "I know and trust Miller. I'll send you a manuscript and you can show it to him."

I mailed off all the stories I had finished and forgot about it.

Four days before Christmas I was standing in my kitchen with my newly pregnant daughter-in-law and my woman divorce lawyer and Bill called to say Miller wanted very much to publish my book of stories.

Nine months later the baby was born and the book was published. It sold ten thousand copies the first week, a really unusual thing for a book published by a university press. They printed it six or seven times. The *Washington Post* gave it a rave review which came out on the day I was doing my first book signing for the book. The party was at Hays and Sanders Bookshop, owned by two of my friends, a poet and a man who is now my colleague in the writing program.

Someone brought the review to the party and showed it to everyone.

I had become a successful, lauded writer. I can't remember much about those years, except the excitement and joy of having fulfilled my childhood dream of becoming a writer, of being part of the world of books.

I am still in awe of those fortunate events, and still love and cherish all the people who helped me along the way.

A month later an agent in New York City named Don Congdon called and asked to represent me. He said an editor at Little, Brown wanted to give me a contract to write a novel and another book of short stories. He said several editors wanted to give me contracts for books but that the most eager one was Roger Donald. "Sure," I said. "I'd love an agent and I'd really like to have a contract and some money."

A few weeks later I flew to New York and met both Don Congdon and Roger Donald. Now I was not only a writer, I was a writer with money and a contract for a book.

I didn't believe much of this. I just liked the excitement and I liked having new friends. Don Congdon is still my agent and Roger Donald was my editor until he retired. Even after he retired he edited two of my books. I'm a small-town girl. I don't table-hop where my life and friendships are concerned.

What else? A really, really good time was had by all.

FEBRUARY 2002

Living in New York City

"MY ONLY ADVANTAGE as a reporter is that I am so physically small, so temperamentally unobtrusive, and so neurotically inarticulate that people tend to forget that my presence runs counter to their best interests. And it always does. There is one last thing to remember: *writers are always selling somebody out*." Every time I have been interviewed I have thought about that quotation from Joan Didion. I did not always think of it immediately and several times I didn't think of it in time to save myself from being misquoted and misunderstood but always in the end I remembered it and drew back from the spin and prevarication that constitutes public discourse in this era of our discontent.

You can't tell reporters anything because they will pick out part of it and use it to tell the story they have decided to tell. They are always looking for *their* story.

In the 1980s I became quasi-famous in the United States and it was the strangest and most annoying thing that has ever happened to me in my life. I had set out to be a poet; my ambition was to write one poem that would stay in the canon for a hundred years and give hope and joy to people when I was dead. Then I started writing fiction and people started paying me for doing it and then I made the mistake of agreeing to be on National Public Radio once a week and bare my soul to the left wing of the American public. This was strange enough since I have always been a conservative, except for the times when I knew a candidate well and worked for him because I wanted to say I knew a governor or a senator or the president of the United States. My main thought after those campaigns were over was that I wished I had my money back.

But I was going to tell you about how I sold out in New York City and agreed to let *Newsweek* and *People* magazine interview me. I had won the National Book Award for Fiction the week before and was going around telling myself I was exceptional and trying to pretend to be an award-winning author. I wasn't sure whether to call myself an author or a writer. I had set out to call myself a poet and didn't know what to do with my new calling and status.

I was living in New York City for the winter, in an overstuffed apartment I had sublet from a wealthy, aging couple from Mississippi I had been introduced to by an actress from Jackson, Mississippi. The apartment was on Second Street between Madison and Park avenues and had a doorman, so I felt like I could sleep safely, but it was filled to the brink with antique furniture and silver and china and old, dusty paintings. It was cleaned twice a week by an aging Scot who had been using the same pile of dust cloths for at least ten years and whose idea of mopping the floors was to add some oil to the dust mop and shine them up.

I fired her after the second visit and moved half of the furniture into the spare bedroom and tried to clear a place where I could work. I got out the ancient vacuum sweeper and used it for several hours until it broke. I hauled it down the street and left it to be repaired at a shop whose name I found on a list in an address book. Then I bought a new vacuum sweeper, hauled it into the apartment and began to clean. I took down the old dusty paintings and put them in the room with the furniture. I stuck posters from the Van Gogh exhibition on the walls with pushpins and decided I could live until spring if only I could get rid of the closet full of dust cloths and oily floor mops. I can't remember whether I threw them away and replaced them with new ones or not. I know when the owners returned they complained that some of their things were missing, and since, besides the vacuum sweeper, I didn't get rid of anything else I suppose I did throw them away.

A month after I fired the maid the owners called and said she needed money so I sent her several hundred dollars in the mail. I was embarrassed that I had forgotten to do it when I fired her but I was so bombarded by the strangeness of living in New York City and having to bring food and firewood into the house via a doorman and an aging elevator that I wasn't working at the top of my form.

This was my state of mind when my editor called and asked me to come to Little, Brown and talk to the "gang" and go to lunch with him at Le Périgord, which is my favorite restaurant in New York City.

When I got to the Little, Brown offices everyone cheered my book award and treated me like royalty and then Roger took me into his office and told me that *People* magazine and *Newsweek* wanted to interview me as soon as possible.

"Of course not," I answered. "I don't like either of those magazines. I might do *Newsweek* if the reporter is someone I respect but I definitely won't be in *People*. It's trash. No self-respecting author would agree to that."

"Oh, you have to do it," he begged. "It's publicity. You can't turn down that kind of thing. They aren't going to write anything bad about you. People just want to know who you are."

"They can read my books," I answered. "I write the books for them. They can have the books. They can't have me. I'm not for everybody."

Roger begged in the taxicab to Le Périgord and he looked sad and agreed to tell them no for me and then he looked even sadder and I remembered he had gone to Andover on a scholarship because his father was poor, so I relented and said I would try to talk to the reporter from *People* magazine but I wasn't sure how much I would tell her about myself.

The next morning she called and asked in a whiny, sad little voice when we could meet. "This afternoon," I suggested. "Come over and see this crazy Victorian apartment I have rented. It's so full of furniture you will think it is a store."

At two that afternoon she showed up at the door. She was a mousy little woman with stringy hair and no makeup and she was clutching a large notebook with pens clipped to the edges of the cover. "I am so physically small, so temperamentally unobtrusive, and so neurotically inarticulate that people tend to forget that my presence runs counter to their best interests. . . ." How had I forgotten that?

We began to talk. She asked if she could use a tape recorder and I agreed and helped her set it up on a table. Such things were more unwieldy and difficult to operate than they are now.

She wanted to know about my childhood. I told her about my powerful, funny, loving father and my wonderful, beautiful mother and my wild, good-looking brothers. I told her about the Mississippi Delta and our plantation, which had been built by the descendants of Yankee soldiers after the Civil War. I told her about my cousins and my friends in Jackson and New Orleans. I told her about New Stage Theatre and Jane Petty and Ivan Rider and Patti Black.

She listened. Then she began to cry. "My mother was a painter," she said. "She was too busy with her work to be interested in me. I never got to go to the country and be on a farm. I never had a happy life." And so on for a long time.

I went over to her and put my arm around her shoulders. I tried to cheer her up but she could not be cheered. She had gone into a decline. After a few minutes of her crying I made tea for her and gave her some of my homemade chocolate chip cookies. Then, in a burst of inspiration, I had an idea. "The Royal Shakespeare Company is playing tonight at Lincoln Center," I said. "They are doing *A Midsummer Night's Dream*. I am going to take you to see it. That will cheer you up." I got on the phone and called Little, Brown and told my editor what was going on. "You got me into this," I told him. "So get us some tickets. I was going tomorrow night anyway. Call me back."

In fifteen minutes he called back and said the tickets would be waiting at the box office at seven that night.

I fed cookies to the poor girl from *People* magazine, then she went home and changed and returned later and I took her to dinner and then to see *A Midsummer Night's Dream* performed by the Royal Shakespeare Company. I could hardly enjoy the play for her being sad in the seat beside me but at least she had stopped crying.

The next week *People* magazine sent a splendid photographer named Thomas Victor to spend ten days following me around and taking wonderful photographs of me all over New York City. He returned on Christmas morning and photographed my entire family who had come to visit me. He gave me *dozens* of fabulous prints of these gorgeous photographs and my family cherishes them. Until his death ten years later, he was one of my favorite people in New York and photographed me many more times, always at someone else's expense.

In late January of 1985 the article came out in *People* magazine. It was all right, but smart-alecky. It tried to make light of my achievements as a writer and was smug and mean-spirited about the South. "See," I told my editor when I had the magazine in my hand. "I told you it was a mistake to talk to this lady."

"Publicity is publicity," he answered. "I think it's very flattering actually."

"Look at the photograph they used," I replied, pointing to a silly, staged photograph of me standing on a bench in Central Park. "Why didn't she use some of the ones that make me look beautiful?"

"That's not how they do it in magazines," he answered. "You should read some of them sometime so you'd know."

"Not in this life," I answered. "I read poetry. I read books."

WINTER 2000

The Sinking Ship

THE WAY YOU START WRITING is by writing. Over and over again I have proven this to myself but I always forget it the next time. I always believe that I will never write again. The first time I finished a book a painter was visiting me. Her name is Ginny Stanford and her wonderful paintings have been the covers for nine of my books.

"I'll never write again," I told her, the week after my editor told me my book was finished and I should quit writing it.

For days after that conversation I had tried to start something new but couldn't think of a thing to write. "That's it," I told the painter. "It's over. It was great while it lasted, but now it's done."

That afternoon she made me a wonderful drawing of a ship sinking in the waves of the sea. "I'll never write again," it said on the bottom of the picture. "September, 1981."

Since then I have published twenty books of fiction, nonfiction, and poetry. Still, I believe it every time. I accept the fact that the part of my life that was writing is over, and I go, at first gingerly, and then wholeheartedly, back into real life. I call my friends, I visit my family, I write letters, invite people to lunch and dinner, buy a new bathing suit, consider risking skin cancer by getting a tan, throw myself into exercise programs, dye my hair platinum blond.

This goes on for weeks or months or even, in its last manifestation, for several years. I write a few magazine articles, perhaps a poem that I throw away, I begin to read again, real books, fiction by people other than myself, or I reread books I have loved.

Then, one day, the germ of an idea begins to enter my head. I begin to see a book before me. I see it mostly in the mornings and maybe I go to the typewriter and make some notes or take a legal pad outside and sit in a sunny chair and make some notes. This is nothing serious, I tell myself, I'm just fooling around. I'm not a writer anymore. Who am I fooling? Maybe I never was a writer. Maybe I was pretending to be one.

Finally, I get the idea in my head that if I write a book I will be paid for it and I could use the money for my grandchildren's education or to help out with a new baby someone in my family is having or to replace my old car or fix the roof. All of this is a lie I tell myself to disguise the fact that I'm dying to start writing again and I don't know if what I'm going to write will be ANY GOOD OR NOT.

That is exactly what my students tell themselves that blocks them from writing. They tell themselves

I DON'T KNOW IF IT WILL BE ANY GOOD OR NOT because it's true. They don't know and the only way they can find out is to do it.

My job as a teacher is tell them that I'll help them make it better if they will grind out a first draft. You don't have to make a home run, I tell them. Just get on first base and I'll knock you in. That is what Frank Stanford told me when he helped me put together my first book of poetry.

But I digress. I want to finish telling you about how the spell of writing comes over me. I tell myself I will get paid, then I call my agent and ask him to get me a contract for a book. He always says he will as if there is no question that anything I write will be welcomed.

Then I start writing in earnest. At first, for the first few days, "it is hard to get back into harness," another thing Frank Stanford told me. I am accustomed to going out to run first thing in the morning. It is difficult to sit at a typewriter instead but I spur myself on with the prospect of being paid and I make myself do it. By the third or fourth day I don't want to go out and exercise. I have started a process and I want to see where it leads. Or else, my unconscious mind has decided to start telling me what I've been thinking and I can't wait to hear what it has to say.

Now my nunlike life kicks in. I stop wearing makeup. I take the phone off the hook. I wear my oldest, most comfortable clothes, I'm careful what I read and who I talk to, I only make appointments in the afternoons and not many of them. I am a writer again and every moment of my life and every breath I take is to prepare me for the time when I wake from sleep and go to my typewriter and serve the muse. There is a muse. She has been with me since my first book. Perhaps she is Athena or the ghost of Edna Millay or maybe the bard himself, walking around London listening to his fellow men and remembering the fields and flowers and seasons of his childhood in Stratford-upon-Avon, or imagining the forest of Arden, which was his mother's maiden name. Is this mysterious or what? You bet it is.

Why do I come back to the typewriter so headily each morning? Because it feels good. The brain is easily addicted to feeling good and nothing on earth, with the exception of great sex, feels as good as having written well and truly in the morning. Actually, it is better than sex because you control the whole activity and the afterglow can last for years if the work is published and other people profit from it. The lasting pleasure is not in their praise but in your knowledge that you have contributed something of value to the culture from which you derive your being.

FALL 2002

Breaking the Rules

RULES ARE MADE TO BE BROKEN. The best thing a writing teacher ever told me was that every time he said something about how to write it ricocheted and came back and hit him in the head. Show, don't tell, always ricochets because every great writer has told us plenty. The work for the young writer is to find the balance. This is the work of the ear. A good writer is a person with a good ear who can hear what the sentence or paragraph is supposed to sound like to the reader. It must ring true to the writer's voice.

Voice, ear, the ability to write is like a singing voice.

Because I believe all of the above I believe young writers should be careful about what they read. I have read great poetry all my life. I am drawn to it. Every morning when I am down at the coast, where I spend half my days, I pick up a book by Robert Frost and read a poem. It is the first thing I do every day and it never fails to cheer me up and teach me and make me wonder at the greatness of Frost and the wonder of nature and the beauty of the seasons. "The force that through the green fuse drives the flower," as Dylan Thomas wrote.

On the coast where I read Frost there are no real seasons. Flowers are always in bloom, leaves are always on the trees, there is almost never any frozen water, the birds don't leave. I think I am reading Frost to remember my other home, up in the Ozark Mountains, which is usually covered with ice when I'm on the coast.

When I am in Fayetteville, Arkansas, which I call my "real" home, I read William Shakespeare every Sunday afternoon with a group of friends. We sit around my dining room table and read the plays out loud. We have become very good at it. At least two of us can pronounce all the names correctly and we almost never stumble over the language as we did when we began this joyous ritual sixteen years ago. Every Sunday afternoon I fill my heart with the greatest writing in the English language. It is also filled with metaphors from nature and the seasons. If I did not live up here where water freezes and leaves fall from the trees I could not understand lines like "Bare ruined choirs, where late the sweet birds sang," or, "Therefore the winds, piping to us in vain,/As in revenge, have sucked up from the sea/Contagious fogs, which, falling in the land,/Hath every pelting river made so proud/That they have overborne their continents . . ." or, "And thorough this distemperature we see/The seasons alter; hoary-headed frosts/Fall in the fresh lap of the crimson rose,/And on old Hiems' thin and icy crown/An odorous chaplet of sweet summer buds/Is, as in mockery, set . . ."

Rules are made to be broken. I tell my students to read great literature. If you want to be television producers, watch television. If you want to be writers, read.

And yet, with the exception of poetry and newspapers, I almost never read while I am writing. If I am deep into a writing project I don't want anyone else's voice to penetrate my unconscious mind. When I am writing I don't like anyone else's writing voice.

Write what you know. Show, don't tell. Writing is rewriting. Don't use modifiers unless they are very special and are earning their way. Question every adjective and question adverbs twice or three or four times. All of those things are probably true most of the time for every writer. A writer who is writing at white heat with the muse at his shoulder doesn't need any rules. All he needs to do is be a good typist.

FALL 2003

In the Weather of the Heart

AN ARCHITECT TOLD ME ONCE, "Write it from the heart and it will be great." I was deep into a book about the friendship between a troubled young mother and a budding architect who was her friend. The book was about my real friendship with the real architect. He had asked me to write it. He was dying. It was his dying wish that I tell some of the stories that we shared.

On the rare occasions when I speak in public, and the even rarer ones when I agree to answer questions about my work, students ask me if my family and friends mind when I use my life as fodder for my work. "Several times they have asked me to write about them," I answer. "My sister-in-law in Alabama once said to me, 'Why do you never write anything about me? I certainly think I've had an interesting life.'" She had two kidney transplants when such things were fairly uncommon. One kidney came from her father and the second one from her mother. The week before the second transplant she and her mother moved into the most expensive hotel in Birmingham, Alabama, and went shopping at the finest stores. Since they are the same size—both are dainty, extremely beautiful women with tiny waists and feet—they figured whoever survived could wear the clothes. When people talk about steel magnolias I always smile to myself over the silly models they use in Hollywood. They should have seen Hilton Hagler and her mother buying shoes the day before they lay down on tables to be transplant subjects.

Another thing Hilton did was marry my brother twice. Both weddings were gorgeous. I was a brides-maid in one and the maid of honor in the second one. Hilton was right. I did owe her a story and I wrote a good one for her. It is called "The Blue-Eyed Buddhist." I left it out of my *Collected Stories* because I thought the ending was too sad but when we redo the book someday I will ask Little, Brown to add it to the stories.

The book about the architect and me when we were young is called *Net of Jewels*. He loved the title and painted a beautiful abstract for me to use for the cover but I couldn't get the art department to use it. The architect had died by the time the book was published and never knew his painting wasn't on the cover. The book is out of print right now. Perhaps when it is reprinted I can get the publisher to use it. Little, Brown has always been my publisher and I have been through many art directors with them. At the moment they have a great one. He would see the beauty of this painting so I will keep my fingers crossed that the book goes back into print while he's in charge.

All of what I have written so far in this essay is to illustrate for young writers as well as I can how very strange and mysterious and yet simple writing really is. At the core of writing is this heart-driven desire to praise, remember, and love. "A process in the weather of the heart," as Dylan Thomas wrote. Most of my teaching is about the outward process of writing, about training for the job, making yourself go back to the typewriter and rewrite, and all of that is helpful to a young writer. But the truth is more beautiful than that. "Write it from the heart and it will be great." A student who wrote a story about trying to protect her younger brother from the bullies on the back of the school bus was writing from her heart. We wept with her, when, against her warnings, the boy kept going back there to take his punishment until he earned his place among the men. She was a young woman with two children and another on the way who had spent most of the last few years cleaning houses for a living. Somehow she had stayed close to her heart, to the real stuff, to what makes us care and weep. I want to lead my students to that place. I want to read what they write when they have found it.

SUMMER 2002

A Writer Should Be Able
to Write Anything

IN THE FALL OF 2001 I created a class called Creative Nonfiction for the graduate students in the writing program. Teaching the fiction workshop the year before had taught me that many of our students would never make a living as fiction writers and should have another outlet for their creative juices. I wanted them to understand that a writer should be able to write anything, poetry, nonfiction, fiction, journalism, papers, letters, love notes.

In order to teach the class I had to reread many of my favorite books. I was trying to choose books that showed the range of possibilities for nonfiction. In the end this is the list I assigned.

Slouching Towards Bethlehem	Joan Didion
The Curve of Binding Energy	John Mcphee
Disturbing the Universe	Freeman Dyson
The World as I See It	Albert Einstein

Pilgrim at Tinker Creek	Annie Dillard
Green Hills of Africa	Ernest Hemingway
Radical Chic &	Tom Wolfe
Mau-Mauing the	
Flak Catchers	

Plus I gave them a long list of recommended books, with emphasis on Truman Capote and Robert Coles.

The book the students liked most was *Slouching Towards Bethlehem*. It inspired two women poets to write some really funny, hard-edged essays that I loved reading and took as much pride in as they did. Three of these essays were published.

A few of the students liked *The Curve of Binding Energy* and others came to like it when the planes flew into the World Trade Center. Several of them told me their first reaction at the terrible news was "what if it is nuclear." I had assigned the book on purpose because I worry that not enough people in the United States understand what nuclear energy is or how uranium-235 and plutonium are manufactured and stored.

Pilgrim at Tinker Creek was inspiring to a few students but the rest found it boring. I was amazed by it when I read it in the seventies but could not recapture that feeling when I reread it for the class. Perhaps Ms. Dillard has been copied so much that we forget what a brilliant thing she did by bringing her poetic skills to explaining nature in contemporary terms and using contemporary science.

I will change my list when I teach the course again next year. It was top heavy with physicists and left out many books that I love. Many of them have disappeared from my library and I am replacing them with the generous "start-up" money given me by the dean when I began to teach. Most new professors use the money to upgrade their computers but I am spending mine on books. Next year I will include *The Snow Leopard* by Peter Matthiessen on my list. And either *African Genesis* or *The Territorial Imperative* by Robert Ardrey. These are seminal books, written by the best writers in their fields. I want my students to read the best and most beautiful writing I can find for them. I'm still searching and reading and ordering books and charging them to the university.

It is difficult to call this work. I must be the luckiest woman in the world to have this job fall into my lap at this time in my life. I should be on my knees every day to thank the world for its blessings.

As Einstein wrote, "A hundred times every day I remind myself that my inner and outer life depend on the labours of other men, living and dead, and that I must exert myself in order to give in the same measure as I have received and am still receiving."

Everyone Wants to Be a Writer

MAYBE I ONLY THINK everyone wants to be a writer because the friends I naturally choose are people who love books. People who love books sooner or later dream of writing them. It's a natural response to stimuli.

Down through the years many lawyers and physicians have come to me with ideas for books. The physicians want to tell me a story and have me write the book. Hired help! The lawyers mostly want to write the book themselves but they want to do it fast and have it published and make a million dollars, or else back to the pursuit of justice.

People have stories they want to tell and that's an honest desire. Wanting to publish a book is mostly about ego, not that ego is bad, it just isn't the thing that drives writing. Writing is driven by the muse. Real writers get into spells when they write, they believe what they write, they are in love with what they write, they will sacrifice for it, give it anything it needs.

My graduate students probably came to the university infused with that spirit but it gets drained out of them by the constant interaction with other writers and the drain on their time of teaching undergraduate composition classes. They are naturally jealous of each other and no matter how hard the smart ones try to keep that at bay it takes its toll. They have to compete for a small number of fellowships and prizes. Plus, they have a difficult time being published. Being an unpublished writer is a terrible Catch-22. You can't get an agent or a publisher interested in your work until you have published and proved you have an audience. So you have to submit stories and poems to small magazines staffed by aspiring writers like yourself. Many of the magazines charge a reading fee to even look at work the students send them.

What can I do to help? How do I fit into this equation? More and more I think the only thing I can do is be the hardest editor they will ever have. Tell them what I know about what I do and how I do it. Show them *on the page* how to edit. Say the same things over and over again. Writing is rewriting. Write what you know. The reward has to be within yourself. Tell the truth about what you know and what you feel. Find out things. Read great literature. Then write. It's only typing. Stop talking about it and do it, or else admit you only want this master's degree so you can teach.

Why am I doing this? Why do I think it will work?

"You Always Use Setbacks to Help You Play Better"

—ANDRE AGASSI

MOST OF MY METAPHORS are from sports. The happiest years of my life were when I was playing tennis all day long in New Orleans. Nothing, not even writing, has ever challenged me as tennis did. I came to the game late in life, in my early thirties, but fortunately I had been running six miles a day for several years so I was in tremendous shape physically when I began to take lessons and learn tennis. I had played on and off as a child but had no real strokes or knowledge of the game. I didn't even know that I had good depth perception or hand-eye coordination. I knew I was from a family of male athletes and by the time I took up tennis I knew enough about heredity and genes to know that women get the same stuff men get, although in different forms.

I write exactly the way I played tennis. I get up at dawn and go at it until noon. Nothing stops me. Nothing is allowed to get in my way. I have hurt the feelings of every good friend I have by needing solitude in which to create. Once I even asked a friend who was visiting me to leave. He had come to stay a week and after four days I asked him to get a hotel room so I could work.

I was on a trip to Europe with friends once and thought of a way to finish a novel I had started so I jumped ship in Switzerland and left them to themselves. The strongest and bravest of my friends have forgiven me these transgressions.

Since I know it is this sort of dedication that makes a writer I know how few of my students will ever achieve what they are seeking in our writing program. Still, I try to believe that by telling them what it took for me to be a successful writer I will make them strong enough to face down their friends and family and take what they need to create.

It was easy for me to do. I didn't seem to have any choice in the matter. For many years my desire to do my work and tell my stories was so intense I would have sacrificed anything to it. I begged forgiveness of the world but I would have continued with my work whether the world agreed to let me do it or not.

I adore watching Andre Agassi play tennis and I love to hear the stories of how he trains for the game. There is a story that he ran up the very high hill he uses for training on Christmas Day. That made sense to me. The best Christmas I ever had was once when my three sons were busy with their women and I was able to spend Christmas week alone finishing my first novel. There was snow and the work was going well and I was as happy as a lark, alone at my typewriter making things come out well for Amanda McCamey and Will Lyons. Later, my editor talked, begged, conned me into changing the ending and letting the book end with the tragic death of Will in an automobile accident. Ten years later I wrote a story bringing him back to life and insisted on putting it into a short story collection. We had never really seen him die in *The Annunciation*, so I had some truck drivers see the accident and run down the hill and save him.

This year, twenty years after the original ending was written, I let Amanda and Will become grandparents. When my copy editor at Little, Brown had that manuscript before him, he wrote me a note. "My God, has it been that long. Seems only yesterday that Amanda was abandoning her Samurai warrior stance to scream for drugs . . ."

In the original ending, the one I wrote that Christmas Day, Amanda gives birth to Will's child while he is driving towards Fayetteville in a snowstorm to tell her he has found the daughter she gave away for adoption years before.

I have had a wonderful time being a fiction writer. I hope I can make it possible for some of my students to do the same.

I must be tough. I must think of Andre Agassi and Steffi Graf, my all-time favorite woman tennis player. I must remember Billie Jean King and Martina Hingis, who goes up against giants with her small five-foot, six-inch frame and wins as often as she loses.

I must think of Coach K at Duke University. My grandson is at Duke and works for the football team so he is in the know on Coach K. Last year, when the Duke team lost to Maryland, Coach K went into the locker room and took out all the benches and took the nameplates off the lockers. He stripped the locker room bare.

When I decide what would be analogous to that in a writing class I will put it into action.

Write What You Know

WRITE WHAT YOU KNOW. What could be simpler, and harder to get a student to believe. A young woman in my undergraduate fiction workshop knows it in her bones. She is a slight, pretty girl with two small children, and, although I did not know it until the class was over, was pregnant with a third the whole time the class was going on. She was quiet, with a charming, small smile. She listened to what I said with great attention. She read the assigned stories and was able to talk intelligently about how they were plotted and where they might have come from in the background of the writer. She was from a rural background and understood Turgenev and Chekhov as I had dreamed young people from farms in Arkansas might understand them.

The first story she wrote for me was a simple tale about a thirteen-year-old girl trying to protect her younger brother from the bullies on the back of the school bus. It began at the rural bus stop where they waited for the bus. It began with a description of the bus as it drew near the waiting children at a crossroads of two country roads.

I can still *see* the story as clearly as the day I first read it. It had such an effect on the class that when they were discussing it everyone was talking at once, telling their own school bus stories. After I read it I began to notice children waiting for buses in the early morning (when I am usually driving to my health club to work out). I became imaginary friends and protectors of two small girls who were always standing at a corner near my house. The older of the two very well-dressed children was always shoving the younger one out into the street. "Stop next time and tell her not to do it or you will call the police," the author of the school bus story told me when I reported my story to the class. "I bet their mother would have a fit if she knew that was going on."

Besides the class being wild with jealousy over the school bus story and filled with their own going-to-school memories, the students were inspired by the school bus story to begin writing all sorts of things about the darkness and blinding light of childhood.

Any thread will lead you out of the darkness and into the light. The school bus woman was our Ariadne. She had shown the class something that all my lecturing had not been able to do. A handsome young man who had been writing stories set on trains in Europe, where he had been once for a month, began to write about his high school basketball team and his work took flight.

You can write stories set on trains in Europe, but only after you learn to praise the world you know in your bones. The older I get the more I read Robert Frost and the more I love his small poems about the seasons.

I have been out of town most of the time since my undergraduate fiction class last semester. Now that I am home I must go and find the young woman who wrote the school bus story and see the baby she was carrying in her womb while she was writing it. It was not the last thing she wrote for me. After the success of the school bus story she wrote at least four more pieces, each equally as lovely and true and funny. I think she could actually become a writer. She was a gift to make me love teaching.

The best thing about the school bus story was the ending. At the end, no matter how the girl tries to keep her brother in the front of the bus where he will be safe, he keeps going back to the dangerous, high testosterone back of the bus and letting the bullies tease and hit him. Finally, he wins the right to sit with them and be a man. The big sister cannot win. Any field biologist could tell her why.

Postscript I

A month after I wrote this essay I ran into the young writer-mother in the hall leading to my office. She had the new baby in a carrier. The baby was on one arm. She had a stack of books of literature in the other arm.

"Oh, please let me see the baby," I said, and she put the carrier on the floor and we both knelt down beside it.

"Is it a boy?" I asked, although I already knew from the clothes.

"Yes. His name is Luther." I looked into the baby's wide, blue eyes. I felt as though I had known him always.

"I've known you since last September, Luther," I told him. "You have lovely eyes.

"Will he be stupid enough to keep going to the back of the bus?" I added, turning back to his mother.

"Who knows?" she answered. "I have three boys and four brothers. You can't tell what any of them might do."

"Keep writing," I said. "You're good at it. I'm in my office on Tuesday and Thursday afternoons. Come and see me."

"I will," she said. "If I have time."

I haven't seen her again, but I am waiting.

Postscript II

I ran into her again this morning at the Fayetteville Athletic Club. She was dressing the children to go to the swimming pool. Divine little boys, towheads with deep blue eyes and the wild energy of their English, Irish, German ancestors, cavemen, inventors, cave painters, Stonehenge builders.

"I'd like to get back to school but as you can see it isn't going to happen soon," she told me.

"You're collecting material," I told her. "Besides, this is the real creation. Everything else is shadow."

"I hope so," she answered and disappeared to the swimming pool.

Choosing the Books

A BIG JOB FOR ANY TEACHER is to choose the books the students read. For a teacher of creative writing it is even more critical that the assigned texts be the best ones. Having no idea how to pick and choose among the riches of literature I began by giving the students books that had influenced me when I began to write.

The testing ground was my first undergraduate course in creative writing II, for which the students supposedly have a strong background in literature. I didn't trust it. Even if they had read Faulkner I was pretty sure they hadn't read what I considered the best of his work.

I have always wondered why most of the anthologies I saw being used in English departments were so bad. They had the right authors in them but not the best work of those authors. My agent told me it is because publishers try to make anthologies out of writings that are in the public domain or can be used for minimal fees. This was such sad information that I went around in a funk for days thinking about it.

I was worried about the cost of the books I assigned the students. Then, standing in line in the university bookstore one day I watched a physics student paying for his books. He paid more for one textbook than the combined cost of everything I had assigned my students.

In the end I assigned a beautiful Library of America anthology of poetry and four paperback books of fiction: *Go Down, Moses* by William Faulkner, *Nine Stories* by J. D. Salinger, *Forty Stories* by Anton Chekhov, and *The Wide Net* by Eudora Welty. Since the purpose of the class was to write, and the books were only to inspire and give examples, I decided that was enough. It was still less expensive than one physics text. I love the sciences and believe in them, but art is my province and natural home and I will defend it now that I am in a position to do so.

It doesn't sound like much of a position. I am an associate professor of creative writing with a BA in philosophy and three honorary doctorates in letters. When I accepted this teaching job they asked me if I wanted to be a full professor and have tenure. I was embarrassed to say yes since I wasn't certain I could do the work so I said no. Since then I have learned that you must have tenure to vote in English department meetings so I wish I'd said yes to that.

But all in all I think I am better off as I am. I don't want expectations to be too high. I am feeling my way into a world I have admired from afar. I'd better watch out for hubris in any form.

This fall will be my third semester of teaching. I am going to be harder this fall and I have changed the books I am teaching the undergraduates. I have found an anthology I like and I am going to teach fiction out of that. It is called *eFictions* and is edited by Joseph Trimmer, Wade Jennings, and Annette Patterson. Besides having the book itself, with its seventy stories, a teacher can order extra stories from a long and amazing list and they will come in bound copies. If I liked I could custom-order copies of the book with the extra stories included or substituted for ones I didn't want.

I am opposed to professors copying stories and giving them to their students as it violates copyright laws. I have done it several times with poetry written by people who are dead but I felt bad about it and won't do it again.

Learning to Teach Writing by Watching a Great Dance Teacher

I HAVE BEEN DOWN on the Mississippi coast for six weeks helping out with six grandchildren who live down there.

My two oldest granddaughters are deeply involved with a wonderful dance studio run by one of the best teachers I have ever watched work in any field. Her name is Donna Burke. She danced professionally and led a dance troupe that danced in Las Vegas thirty years ago. She was trained in classical ballet and teaches it the old-fashioned way.

I discovered Donna ten years ago and flew down to the coast and enrolled my granddaughters in her school. Then I bought a condominium in the town where they live so I could be there to drive them to their classes. They longed to dance and I longed to help them do it. I had only sons. The chance to help my granddaughters learn to dance was too seductive to miss.

My mother had enrolled me in dance classes several times but I didn't have the right personality to put up with the discipline. Neither do my granddaughters really but, luckily, Donna's School of Visual and Performing Arts is the main game in the small town of Ocean Springs, Mississippi. Most of the girls who get elected cheerleader or win the beauty contests or are on the homecoming court are Donna's students. It's a leg up in a tough, competitive world and my granddaughters knew it. Peer pressure was on my side and so for ten years I have had the pleasure and pain of watching Donna work on my hardheaded progeny.

Donna takes no prisoners. She accepts no excuses. Being late to class or improperly dressed or missing a rehearsal is not an option. Praise is rare and hard-earned. Hard work earns you more hard work and higher expectations. The result is that her studio has won DANCEAMERICA national competitions three times and so many other trophies that the wall of shelves will not hold them all. They are piled on top of one another and covered with dust. There is no time for dusting trophies at Donna's studio. Past accomplishments are nothing. The coming recital or competition is all. This seems very Zen to me. I can sit on the floor and watch Donna conduct rehearsals for hours.

I know genius when I see it and I am thrilled to have been able to give my granddaughters a taste of it.

This year, after ten years of work, they are on Donna's competition team and rehearsing for their first competition in April. Besides the three regular two-hour classes they take after school on Tuesdays, Wednesdays, and Thursdays, they have extra rehearsals on Saturday mornings and sometimes on Sunday afternoons.

The results are high school dance teams that look like professional dancers. It is amazing what Donna and her helpers have done with small groups of girls on the Mississippi coast. If you ever wonder "why all those writers come from Mississippi," just go and watch Donna's dancers getting ready for a competition or a recital.

What does all this have to do with my teaching creative writing? Well, this fall my students are going to profit from the hours I have spent watching Miss Donna rehearse the competition team. I have been too easy on my students these first two years of my apprenticeship. I have let them get away with sloppy manuscripts and delays and all sorts of things I would never put up with in my own work.

My students have come to me to learn to become published writers. "What you do in practice you will do in performance," I have heard Donna say a thousand times. The same is true in writing.

"I want that revision tomorrow," I'm going to start telling my students. "I didn't spend my time editing that story to have you sit on it for weeks. Go home and fix it now."

This fall I am going to feel the spirit of Donna Burke's consummate professionalism in me as I teach.

I'm going to remember her courage and backbone and unrelenting drive to excellence and demand from my students what she demands from hers.

Many of her students quit. Each year I have to drive my youngest granddaughter back into her classes and I don't mean in my automobile. "Just one more year," I tell her. "Just until Christmas. Just until you make the competition team. Just until you get your toe shoes. You don't have to, of course, but how can you quit now?"

The thing I need to learn from Donna is that I am the teacher. I'm not there to get the students to like me or think I'm nice. I'm there to show them what it takes to succeed.

In a university that means you have to put up with them complaining to the head of the department or the dean and writing nasty things about you on the student evaluations at the end of the semester.

I don't know if I'm brave enough for this job but I'm going to pretend to be. Hold me to this if you are around next semester at the University of Arkansas in Fayetteville.

Crisis in the Creative Writing Program

WE ARE LOOKING FOR A POET to take the place of a poet/novelist/teacher/founder of the program/defender of the program against all intruders, including the English department, the dean, and the university of which we are a part.

The man we need to replace is named Jim Whitehead and he is the strongest man any of us has ever known. He is six feet, seven inches tall, has seven children, married the most beautiful woman in Mississippi, published a novel in his twenties, created this writing program, and has watched over it for forty years. He has fought for its independence from the English department, the dean, and all interference of any kind from the rest of the university.

This is my first hiring experience as part of the creative writing faculty and I think it is worth including as part of this book. I don't know how I thought such things were achieved. I suppose I thought you just found someone and asked them to come work with you.

We are supposed to fill Jim Whitehead's shoes and the dean has only given us six months for the search. We are limping because we don't have a poet. Our woman poet, Enid Shomer, is on medical leave and is in New York City fighting cancer and having back surgery. We don't know when she can return. Our famous, founding poet, Miller Williams, is retiring but has agreed to stay one more year. Our third poet is on sabbatical and is in China. In the meantime our best young student poet has left the program and the rest of the poets are applying to other writing schools. Because I believe that poetry is the heart of language I am deep into the search even though I am not teaching this semester.

Our first choice to fill Jim Whitehead's shoes is a slight, quiet young man from Kentucky who is very different from Jim. His name is Davis McCombs. He spent the seven years after he graduated from Harvard being a park ranger in Mammoth Cave in eastern Kentucky. While there he wrote a book of poems about the cave, seen partly through his own eyes and partly through the eyes of a black slave who was the guide in the cave in the early years after its discovery. The book of poems is mysterious and wise and philosophical and tender. It is about wandering in the interior of the earth. There is no resentment in the book, only wonder and tenderness and love.

Most of the manuscripts from our other candidates are about their own interior spaces. I will learn from this to demand from my students that they go out into the world and find something to write about besides their own problems.

Meanwhile we have to hire a poet. My choice is Davis McCombs. He was a student of Seamus Heaney's while at Harvard. Maybe that made the difference. Or maybe he is by nature a careful, thoughtful man who sees beyond himself and knows that life is mysterious and good.

Postscript I

It is two years since I wrote the beginning of this piece. Davis McCombs is part of our faculty and has been as wonderful in his quiet way as the fiery Jim Whitehead was in his. We have lucked up in the poet department, that's for sure. Our best poet has returned to the program. Another poet won our second Wallace Stegner fellowship in as many years. Enid Shomer has survived her ordeal. Things are looking up. As a fiction and creative nonfiction teacher I need poets. I like to turn them into double agents if I can.

Postscript II

Jim Whitehead died two days ago. It was sudden, shocking. We are in mourning in Fayetteville, Arkansas.

AUGUST 2003

Everyone Thinks They
Are a Writer

SINCE I BEGAN TEACHING I have begun to get telephone calls from people who are dear to me, mostly
men and mostly lawyers, but a medical student also
called, asking me questions about how to write short
stories. "How long does one have to be?" the medical
student asked, but it turned out what he really wanted
to know was how many pages you needed altogether to
make a book and get paid for it.

It is as if, after years of being very close and secre-
tive about my work, I have opened up to share what I
know with the world and my close friends have sensed
it is all right to ask me to tell *them* while I'm at it. It is
very strange to feel this sea change in me, this unac-
customed unselfishness. All these years I have thought
that other writers were competition and I wouldn't go
on the practice court with them because I might meet
them in a slam and they'd know my moves. Now,
because I am being paid for it and because it has turned
out to be a joy, I am willing to train my competition,
maybe even, someday, rejoice if they best me.

This opening up, this unselfishness, is very wonderful. I am naturally an unselfish person, but where my work was concerned I was as tight as my deepest Scot ancestor in his mountain hold.

But it isn't selfishness alone that makes me not want to talk about my work. It's a kind of shyness, something I don't really understand. My work is my refuge, my hideout. Occasionally I like to talk about it but mostly I don't. Now, for some reason, I am becoming more open. A reporter described me recently as "an extroverted recluse." I felt the description was apt. When I am working I am as disciplined and closed-up as a nun on a retreat. When I am finished for the day I like to dress up and go downtown and see what's going on but I don't go to my friends. I go to the mall and walk around and look at strangers or wander into toy stores and buy presents for my young grandchildren or go by the cosmetic counter and ask the Chanel representative about the new antiwrinkle compounds. I want to completely leave myself when I reenter the world and my friends would ask me questions about where I've been.

I don't want to answer questions about the strange, quiet place where I dream and write. "What are you writing now?" is a terrible question to me. I don't want to talk about it while I'm doing it. That's the end of that.

When something comes up in a class that involves a student's work and I can help the student by giving him or her an example from my own work, it is different. I initiated the revelation and since I am the teacher I can cut off the discussion if I don't like where it's going. Is this about power? If I like power it's news to me but it could be true. I'll be watching to find out.

Why Is Rewriting So Hard?

WHY IS REWRITING SO HARD? Why is it so hard to talk yourself into going back to a first draft and working on it? Why is it so hard to get started? Why do we procrastinate and procrastinate over this? I say WE on purpose because the main thing my students have taught me is that every writer seems to have the same problem. Here I am, twenty books and hundreds of magazine articles later, supposedly a grown woman, and when an editor sends me back a manuscript to have even small changes made, I go around in a huff for hours or maybe even days before I can sit down and get the work done. I would never rewrite anything unless I needed to make money.

I have thought about this long and hard since I have been teaching. Why do the students get that expression on their faces when told something has to be CHANGED? Why do I feel such trepidation when I open an envelope containing a manuscript returned to me from a LOVING editor who has been WORKING ON IT?

There is only one explanation that seems possible to me. We are all perfectionists and we can't stand to think we did something wrong EVEN IF WE KNOW HOW TO FIX IT AND DO IT RIGHT THE SECOND TIME. This is so childish. The expression on my students' faces when they don't want to go back to work is childish. My huffiness over editing is childish. It must be our parents' fault. Off with their heads.

Metaphorically we do have to assassinate the parents within us, whatever nasty, complaining, correcting voices we hear. When we let another person read a manuscript we want complete and instant praise. The artist is a two-year-old child. She does not want to be criticized in any way. That's what you have to deal with to be a writer. You have to love and nourish the child within who writes the stuff. You have to give the little witch chocolate candy and feed her nasty little ego and then you have to get tough and tell her to sit down at the desk and act like a man or there won't be any money for next month's trip to the mall.

Except the students don't get money or publications and threatening to give them bad grades just makes the problem worse. Publish anywhere you can, I tell them. Get your name in print. Show the publications to your family and friends. Don't be a would-be author. It's too sad. Write things, rewrite them, get published anywhere. Or else, find something else to do. Don't pretend you are a writer. Be a writer.

Then I give them *On Writing*, a collection of small bits of advice by Ernest Hemingway. Once I copied a piece of it and put it on the first page of the worksheet. This is hard talk about a difficult profession but I thought they needed to hear it.

> *First there must be talent, much talent. Talent such as Kipling had. Then there must be discipline. The discipline of Flaubert. Then there must be the conception of what it can be and an absolute conscience as unchanging as the standard meter in Paris, to prevent faking. Then the writer must be intelligent and disinterested and above all he must survive. Try to get all these in one person and have him come through all the influences that press on a writer. The hardest thing, because time is so short, is for him to survive and get his work done.*
>
> —ERNEST HEMINGWAY

Sunday Morning

TEACHING IS MAKING ME examine my work habits, the obsessive-compulsive patterns that I create or fall into.

Take this morning for example. I rose with the sun as always, made coffee, folded some laundry, made the bed, and then started into my workroom to reread parts of this book that I have already written.

I didn't make it to the workroom for another half hour. First I began to think about my father's Auburn class ring and how it became too large for him when he was old. My onyx class ring is getting too large for me. I have always worn it on my left hand as it helps me tell my left from my right. Now I keep taking it off and putting it down in odd places where I will sooner or later probably lose it.

Then I began to think about my mother, bedridden in a nursing home in Jackson, Mississippi, and still an angel in every way. Then I stood at a window for a long time looking at the trees just putting out their first spring buds. How beautiful the world is this morning. I wanted to be out taking a long walk in its awakening beauty but I had sworn to get seriously back to work.

Then I started thinking about the Episcopal Church and how much I missed the liturgy and the music and the strange ritual of early morning communion, the taste of wine and the beautiful language written in the time of Shakespeare and Ben Jonson. I got out a phone book and looked to see what time early communion begins at Saint Paul's Episcopal Church, which is a few blocks from my house. The minister there is John Grisham's first cousin and is much beloved in this town. Many of my friends have joined or returned to the church because of him.

I definitely decided to put on a suit and go down and take communion in honor of my father and my mother and to see if it still gives me the peace and good feeling it did when I was young. The wonderful thing about early communion is that there is no sermon, nothing human to stand in the way of the gorgeous language of the King James version of the Bible.

So I may leave my work and go to church instead of rereading my essays. Why don't I want to work this morning? I think it is because I'm not certain the book will ever be published. I am accustomed to having advances for books, being paid for the work before the work is done. If I want that for this book I must show part of it to a publisher and see if they want to buy it. "You consign the pot to the fire and you accept the judgment of the fire," potters say. It is true of writing also.

I must remember to tell my students about this morning. The self-doubt and then finding something to blame and then, luckily, coming to my senses and going back to work. I love the Episcopal Church and honor the work they do for children and homeless people but I don't believe the theology. I am acting when I take communion. I don't believe the wine and bread represent anything but wine and bread. My allegiance is to the work at hand.

It is a crapshoot to write and that is that. I will probably get a contract for this book and be paid a reasonable advance but I haven't gotten it yet because I haven't done enough work to merit it. This is the truth of my profession. You have to create something out of nothing and hope someone will pay you to keep doing it so you can pay the rent. I never encourage anyone to be a writer except the students who have already committed themselves to this craziness. Many members of my family have the verbal skills and creative imagination that have made me a writer but I never encourage them to do it. "Never tell anyone to be a writer," Eudora Welty once said. "It's too hard to do."

My younger brother put it best. I was answering his questions about how a writer is paid and how much they earn and so forth. He is a businessman and was checking to find out if I was okay. After I answered all his questions he sighed and shook his head. "That's a tough racket you're in, honey. Are you sure you want to do that for a living?"

The way I talked myself into going back to work that Sunday morning was poetry. The real reason I gave up the idea of going to church was remembering Wallace Stevens's poem "Sunday Morning." "Why should she give her bounty to the dead?/. . . . Shall she not find in comforts of the sun,/In pungent fruit and bright, green wings, or else/In any balm and beauty of the earth,/Things to be cherished like the thought of heaven?"

After I thought of that, I got up from the bed where I was lying, poured fresh-squeezed orange juice into a glass and went back to work. "It's hard to get back into harness," the poet Frank Stanford once told me, meaning getting back into the routine and work habits that are the bedrock of a writer's life.

But I am good at doing hard things. The old daddy I miss so much got up at dawn every day and did his work and I will do mine also.

How can this knowledge help my students? Perhaps I will Xerox this and give it to them this fall. Then I will threaten to give them really bad grades if they don't meet my deadlines for stories. Deadlines, bylines, and a pay check. Those are things a writer needs and why I think an apprenticeship in journalism is a good place for a writer to make a beginning. Is a writing school a good place for a writer? I am making up my mind as I teach in one. I learned to write short stories in this school but I didn't stay very long. Maybe it is different for each student. The very talented ones should take what we have to teach and move on out into the big world as soon as possible. I believe that because it's what I did twenty-five years ago and it worked for me.

Eudora Welty

MY MOTHER IS ALIVE and her mind is clear but her body is failing. She will be ninety-five years old in a few weeks. For three years she has been bedridden and now she is almost unable to move. It is very painful for me to visit her. I love to look into her eyes and talk to her, which is as it always has been. But to watch the terrible invasions she must undergo to be cared for breaks my heart.

I tell you this because it reminds me of the year I was lucky enough to be in the only classes Eudora Welty ever taught. That year her beloved mother had been put into a nursing home near Jackson, Mississippi. Eudora's friends in the English department at Millsaps College had talked her into teaching a creative writing workshop to help cheer her up as she nursed her mother. Also, probably, to help defray the costs of the nursing home. This was a low point in Eudora's career. She had not published a book in many years and was struggling with the long novel *Losing Battles*, which was about the lingering last years of a matriarch in the country. Of course, it was a metaphor for what Eudora and her family were going through. Eudora, with her brilliant imagination, had turned her small, almost dying family into a large, laughing clan with lots of powerful young men. In her own family one brother had already died and the other one was ill. Eudora did have two wonderful, strong nieces and I think I see them in the beautiful young women in the novel.

I think often of that year I spent with Eudora. Her kindness and maturity were the main things I loved about her. She was like my mother and almost the same age. It seemed hard to imagine that the kind, gentle woman who climbed the steps of the Millsaps library two afternoons a week to talk to us was a famous writer. When she talked about literature, about stories she loved, then I believed it, but not when I saw her coming up the steps with her hunched back and wearing her little stocking cap and looking so sad. She drove to the nursing home every afternoon and spent the evening with her mother.

Tomorrow I am getting in the car to go and spend two days with my mother. The drive I have to make is much longer than the one Miss Welty made but the expression on my face is the same one she wore as she climbed the steps to our classroom. I hope we cheered her up as much as my students cheer me up. They take me out of myself. They present me with problems to solve and I try to solve them.

Yesterday I had a note in my mailbox asking me to recommend a young woman to the graduate school of education. She was the worst student in my class last year and contributed nothing to the workshop. Half the time she had not read the stories we were going to talk about. Yet I liked her for being honest. "I haven't read this" was all she would ever say when I called on her. Also, she was always there, on time, and always listening to everything I said. And she turned in her work on time.

I agonized over what to say in the letter I wrote to the education school. Finally I wrote that she was dependable and honest and very shy about talking in class. I think that was basically true. I told the person to whom I was writing that she didn't talk in class but I thought it was because she was overwhelmed by the powerful students who were extremely opinionated and critical. After I wrote the letter I decided I believed it. Teaching is turning out to be a lot deeper than I thought at first. Layers upon layers. No wonder no one ever gets any writing done after they begin to teach. At first I didn't understand that but the longer I teach the more I understand why it happens.

Another Hard Thing for a Writer to Learn to Handle

YOU CAN'T BE A PUSSY in this game, which is why I assign Ernest Hemingway's *On Writing* to every class I teach. It is a collection of small pieces of writing advice that are scattered around his books and letters. It has been an invaluable help to me in the years I have been writing. It reminds me to be strong and to know that what I am doing has never been easy for anyone. If you want an easy profession find one that has a more dependable source of income and praise.

The great thing about writing is that you are self-employed. The bad thing about writing is that you have to wait on other people to find out if you are going to be published. Then, you have to wait to find out if anyone is going to buy the book, or like it, or read it, or keep it in print.

A writer cannot afford to spend much time thinking about all of that. A writer is a person who writes, who continues to create, who believes he can create and that the world is so full of material that if we all wrote all the time we would never begin to use it up.

Here is the process that leads to publication. You think of something to write and you start writing it. You don't know exactly what you're doing. You don't have a blueprint or a map. You are taking a line for a walk, as an artist once said about drawing.

Sometimes this process catches fire. Sometimes it doesn't. The longer you work as a writer the more likely you are to know which is which and you learn to abandon the projects that aren't leading anywhere.

When something does catch fire, when the muse appears and the work is going well and you can't wait to get back to the typewriter each morning, to FIND OUT WHAT IS GOING TO HAPPEN NEXT, then you begin to think about showing what you are doing to your editor or agent. In my case my editor and agent are close friends and trust each other so sending work to my agent includes them both. If he thinks it is good enough he will send it right over to my editor.

Then the wait begins. If the work is good I will know it and not worry too much about whether they are going to like it. I should worry about whether what I sent them is something they can sell to my publisher or something the publisher can sell to the public but I can't afford to think about that. I have to follow my heart, write what I know or believe or dream or am interested in and hope it turns out well.

What am I supposed to do while they are reading the work I have sent them? Keep on writing as if it didn't matter. I usually send about sixty pages of a manuscript to them. If it is a novel I will include an outline of what I think the rest of the book will be. If it is short stories I only send the stories. In the case of this book it will be about twenty small essays.

Then I wait. I am waiting now. But I am not worried about this book. It is something I have wanted to write for years. I want to help young writers. I want to help aspiring writers. I want to help the writer I was when I was forty years old and gave up drinking and decided to settle down and use my talents.

I have thought on and off for years about writing this book but I could not get started. I couldn't find an entry into the material. Then I began to teach, thinking I would never write again and happy to quit. The first semester that I taught I wrote a book of stories that I love. The second semester I wrote nothing but I began to make notes for these essays, thinking they might be of use someday.

This is the process in the weather of the mind. This is how you wait for lightning. "A poet is someone who stands out in rainstorms all his life and once or twice gets struck by lightning," Randall Jarrell once wrote. I was solaced by that when I began writing. I am solaced by it now.

But what if the manuscript you send your editor isn't good enough? What if it is a terrible mess like the first draft of *The Annunciation* that I mailed to New York City in November of 1981? I had never written a novel or wanted to write one but Little, Brown had given me an advance for one on the basis of a book of short stories I had written the year before that had a big success after it was published by a university press.

I didn't question why they wanted a novel. They had offered me fifty thousand dollars to write one which was a huge sum in 1981 so I set to work to do it.

I had no idea how bad the manuscript was that I sent them in November, but I remember it was very long. Three or four hundred pages of rambling description and dialogue, with many asides and quotations and too many characters. Later I burned hundreds of pages of manuscript that led up to the book I finally published. I am not sorry that I burned it. I can't imagine a time when I would want to read it again.

Poor Roger Donald, my editor, and poor Don Congdon, my agent. They had taken my success and turned it in a direction it didn't want to go and they probably knew it as they tried to deal with the manuscript I had sent them. I remember Don telling me on the phone one day that I must remember this was not a movie, there was no actress performing *The Annunciation*, and I had to make my central character real ON THE PAGE.

But that was later. First the manuscript was sent to Roger Donald, then silence fell. Thanksgiving went by, then Christmas, with not a word from New York City about my book. If I had known then what I know now I would have tried to start writing something else but I was new to publishing so I just sweated it out. "They have you on tenterhooks," my psychoanalyst told me. "Call them up and tell them to report to you. Then take your boyfriend and go somewhere for a vacation. Change the venue."

Luckily I was in love so I took my boyfriend and we went up to Eureka Springs and spent a week at a small resort on a mountain lake. We built fires and made love and ate wonderful meals in German and Italian and French restaurants but I was suffering terribly. I called Roger many times. Sometimes he returned the calls. Sometimes he didn't.

Deep inside myself I must have known how bad the manuscript was and now I would recognize that feeling, but then I needed someone to blame so I blamed him for my distress.

Think of it from his point of view. He had discovered a new writer and given me a lot of money to write another book and the book I sent him was a mess. This happens all the time, I have learned in the years since, but then I thought I was the first person in the world to suffer such distress.

There was a happy ending. By the end of January Roger had managed somehow to edit the thing and mailed it back to me and Don Congdon got on the phone and healed and coached me and they both told me I could do it and I went back into the manuscript and rewrote it and made it better and then they edited it again and then I rewrote it again and by the end of the summer I had finished the book.

In May of 1983 it was published. It got bad reviews and sold sixty or seventy thousand copies. Since then it has sold about six hundred thousand copies in different editions, been optioned for the movies twice and made me a lot of money and earned me a lot of fans. It's not a great novel but it's a good read and people like it and keep telling other people to read it.

In the wake of all that distress I went happily back to writing short stories and wrote *Victory Over Japan*, for which I won the National Book Award for Fiction in 1984.

Lucky me. I have always been lucky in my work. Lucky in the wonderful men and women who have taught and helped me on my way. Don Congdon and Roger Donald and Bill Harrison, who taught me how to write the short story, and Eudora, and the muse, and my family who put up with the stories I tell.

How I Invented Traceleen

FIRST, I LEARNED to love a woman who was very different from me. On the day I moved to New Orleans my mother-in-law sent a lovely black woman named Rosalee over to my house to help me move and, if we liked each other, to become my housekeeper. Her aunt worked for my mother-in-law and she was working there part-time as a laundress. She was adept at ironing button-down Brooks Brothers shirts until they looked like objects of art. She was very beautiful, quiet and gentle and ladylike. She reminded me always of a dancer. She moved with grace and she brought beauty and grace into my life.

She was the mother of three small children and was in the process of getting an unhappy divorce from their father. She came to my house four days a week around ten in the morning and stayed until the afternoon. She was so good at everything she did that she was often finished early and went on home. If her children were ill or needed her, it was fine with me if she stayed at home. I was appalled at what a small sum of money she was accustomed to making and quickly began paying her as much as I could. My husband was generous about this. Finally, after her divorce, and after I visited her in the project and was appalled at the conditions there, my mother and I lent her the money to make a down payment on a small house. I loved Rosalee and she loved me. Whatever anyone wants to say about the fact that she was the maid and I was the employer is their problem. We were not into that sort of thing. We liked each other. We came to love each other and we helped each other and we had a good time working together to make life better for both our families.

My husband and I had learned to scuba dive and we would go off on trips for several weeks at a time to islands in the Caribbean to try out different reefs. While I was gone on these trips Rosalee got into the habit of writing down what was happening on *As the World Turns*, a soap opera we both watched every day. I don't remember whose idea it was for her to write down the events of *As the World Turns*. I think she just started doing it to be nice. At that time there was no *Soap Opera Digest* or plot summaries in the newspapers.

Some years later, when I had just begun writing short stories, I was in the bathtub in my house in Fayetteville, Arkansas, and I heard a voice saying, "Another time, Miss Crystal did a real bad thing at a wedding." It was the voice Rosalee used to write down the plot of *As The World Turns*. I jumped out of the tub, threw on a red towel, ran to my typewriter and began to write the first Traceleen short story. I was laughing the whole time I was writing the story and I still think it is funny. I was seeing my own crazy, obsessive behavior through the eyes of the most nonjudgmental person I had ever had as a friend.

Unfortunately, I allowed my editor to talk me into changing the first line of the story when I put it into *Victory Over Japan*, but I restored it for my *Collected Stories*.

God bless Rosalee Harris for her goodness and kindness to me in real life and for her generosity in allowing me to model a character after the divinity of her being. I love Rosalee and always will and I love Traceleen and Miss Crystal, even though they are pale shadows of their progenitors. There are a lot of real stories I could never tell.

How to Move Characters from One Place to Another

IF YOU WANT TO LEARN how to make characters move around and do things, open up *Huckleberry Finn* to any page and start reading. No one does it better than the old master, Mark Twain. One night I was driving to Nebraska in a rainstorm and turned on the radio to keep me company as I drove through the wheat fields of Kansas. I tuned into a station that was playing a recording of *Huckleberry Finn*. I started listening at the point where most readers stop paying attention in the book, the part where Huck and Tom have Jim hidden out in a shed although they know he has already been freed by Tom's aunt.

It was fascinating. I forgot that I was all alone on a highway in a storm and had no place to stay for the night. I forgot I didn't have a map and wasn't even sure I was on the right road. I was cheering for Huck to get up the courage to tell Tom they had to tell Jim the truth and let him go home.

First you have to create characters that are more real than real people. Then you have to let them talk like real people, even if you have to face down the language police to do it. Then you have to think up things for them to do that are the sort of stories that would make you buy the morning paper to find out what happened in the end. A great writer like Mark Twain will give you so much information that anyone with brains could figure out what will happen eventually but still keep you spellbound as you wait to find out how and when it will happen.

You write your way into a character or characters. You cannot think up characters or outline them. You have to write them in action with other characters. William Shakespeare knew Hamlet for a long time before he brought him full-blown into his own play. The first we hear of Hamlet is through the conversation of two of his friends, Marcellus and Horatio. "Let us impart what we have seen tonight/Unto young Hamlet, for upon my life,/This spirit, dumb to us, will speak to him," the good Horatio says. The playwright knows his central character so well that even this first mention is charged with meaning and with power.

In the next scene we are in the crowded court and after hearing requests from other characters the king turns to a black-suited Hamlet standing apart and speaks to him. "But now, my cousin Hamlet, and my son—"

Hamlet answers in an aside to the audience. "A little more than kin, and less than kind." Already, in his first speech he has distanced himself from the court and made the audience his friend. Later, when he speaks his great monologues we will not be surprised.

Shakespeare had written the play once before. He knew his character well.

I tell my students that one story does not exhaust a character's possibilities for a writer. I discovered this by doing it. It seemed natural to me. When I was a child I had loved series of books having the same main character and I still do love them. Sometime last year I discovered John le Carré and devoured all his books. I especially loved the ones about the master spy, George Smiley.

The year before that I discovered Tony Hillerman and read the books until three in the morning for a month. I sent them by Federal Express to a lawyer friend who is part Chickasaw Indian and he was reading them as fast as I was. I was spending the night at his house recently and we began talking about that wonderful six weeks when we read Tony Hillerman instead of sleeping. "It was so good," I said.

"I wish we could find some more books that good," he answered, and we sighed, as though in memory of a great, lost love.

"Let's read them again," I said.

"Yes," he agreed. "Let's start right now."

I took his copy of *Coyote Waits* and went up to the guest room and got in bed and started reading. A reader doesn't ask much of the writer but the one thing all readers want is more of a good character. The books don't all have to live up to the standard of the first one. We just want to know more, as much as the writer will give us. When Larry McMurtry wrote *Duane's Depressed* a few years ago, catching us up on the hero of *The Last Picture Show* and *Texasville*, I almost sent him flowers. Thank you, thank you, generous writer.

You create characters by writing about them until you know them. Write down who their great-grandparents were and where they lived and what they did for a living. Tell me what the hero's mother cooked for dinner and how long she lived and if she yelled at him or indulged him. How many siblings did he have? Where are they now? What did he think about when he was seven, eight, nine, ten? Did he play sports? Did he go to church? What was his favorite food? What did he get for Christmas when he was ten?

You have to know all of that and so much more. You don't have to use it, but you have to know it.

Create characters. Think up something for them to do. Start writing. Tell the story and be sure to make it ring true. Believe in the story your imagination gives you. Stick to it. Don't worry about what anyone is going to think when they read it. They will never read it unless you want them to.

How to Become Inspired

YOU CAN PRIME THE PUMP, which seldom gives very good results. You can need money; this will work but it's not the absolute best way. You can read great literature and hope you'll want to write an answer. Or, best of all, you can be inspired by something the world does to you or for you or that you notice. Today I was inspired by something that has never done it for me before. I was inspired to write a short story by reading a review of my *Collected Stories* that made me laugh out loud three times. I was laughing at my own stuff and at the reviewer's very funny reaction to it.

I had forgotten I had written the things she was quoting. They were so silly I couldn't believe anyone would write them. Where on earth did I get the moxie to write things so absurd and true? Of course it is because I do absurd, compulsive things and I know they are funny when I do them. I do them to make myself laugh and I was probably still laughing when I wrote them down and am still laughing. Carpe diem. I invented the behavior.

How can such knowledge about my own work help my students? I don't know. I tell them all the time, "If you think it's funny, it is funny. If it makes you laugh, it will make the reader laugh. Trust yourself, especially about humor. Humor is the highest art form. Satire, irony, whatever you choose to call it. If you think it's funny, the reader will too. Don't second-guess the highest form intelligence takes and for God's sake, don't edit it. Trust it, love it, keep it."

Here's how this inspiration began. I was watching a tennis tournament on television. I wasn't looking for inspiration or thinking about doing any serious writing. At three in the afternoon I decided to go out to the mailbox, telling myself that going to the mailbox was probably not worth the trip. The check a speakers' agency in New York owes me won't be there. I will get advertisements of credit, notices of sales at Talbot's, discount coupons from Pier One, manuscripts I will never read and solicitations from people wanting me to do things they think up that I don't want to do and won't do unless they pay me for doing them.

I got all of the above, no check, and a fat envelope from Little, Brown with reviews of the paperback edition of my *Collected Stories*.

I threw all the junk mail away and put the reviews on the dining room table for later. Much later, while I was watching the semifinals of the NASDAQ 100 tennis tournament in Miami, I put the reviews beside my recliner to read during advertisements or times when the match got too tight and I couldn't bear to watch anymore. That wasn't going to happen this night anyway because it was Serena Williams against Jennifer Capriati and I didn't care which one of them won.

During the first break, when they were still on serve, I picked up the reviews and began reading them. I don't usually read reviews. I just sort of look them over to see if they are well-intentioned or not.

I was really reading these, especially the one that later inspired me to write. It was a brilliant, funny piece by a woman named Susan Miller Williams for the *Women's Review of Books* at Wellesley College. It was beautifully written and wonderfully funny. I just laughed and laughed and then, a little later, I went to bed and slept like a baby, still basking in the glow of laughing at my own work and being pleased by having been praised by a good writer.

I got up the next morning and wrote the first seven pages of a funny, outrageous story about a woman my own age who takes a lover, breaking all her vows not to have sex that has to be chemically augmented.

What does all that mean for someone who wants to know how to become inspired? I think it means you have to be living a life full of other interests besides writing at the same time that you are writing every day whether you are inspired or not. If you are in the habit of writing down your thoughts you will have the basket waiting when the inspiration manna starts falling from heaven.

There I go again, articulating things I thought could not be articulated.

My students think they have to travel to remote parts of the world to have material to write about. The male students think they are missing out if they never got to go to a war. I am glad they want to go out and see the world but many great writers never traveled far from where they were born. Shakespeare, Turgenev, Eudora Welty, William Faulkner, the list goes on and on.

At one level inspiration is the ability to see beauty and mystery in everything men and women do. That may be a gift not everyone has.

Decons

I HAVE BEEN WATCHING the deconstructionists in the English department and I've decided it's an occupational hazard. They study and teach the same short stories or novels over and over again until they begin to obsess about them. They need to add to them, explain them, pull them apart and carry the pieces around and show them to each other. They have conferences in Lyon, France, and pull apart Eudora Welty's stories, conferences in Oxford, Mississippi, and sit in panels to dissect Faulkner's novels.

They can't leave it alone. Instead of calling all their fellow Welty lovers together and saying, listen, I'm going to read you something wonderful and reading *The Ponder Heart* or "The Wide Net" or "A Worn Path" out loud, leaving their listeners full of beauty and mystery and music, they start talking about Uncle Daniel's dysfunctional family or why Doc lived all alone in the country. Come on. It used to make me mad when I was not near academia and only had to watch this sad silliness from afar. Now it makes me sad because some of the people who are doing it are the nicest, most hardworking people in English departments in universities that I love.

Every one of them is a frustrated writer who can't get up the will or whatever it is that lets real writers stay up all night making up stories and poems. They usually are people who wanted to write and gave it up in the face of greater talents. They are good people. They don't waste the rest of their lives in jealousy. They hook up with some writer or group of writers they like to read and become experts on something that doesn't need expert help.

All you need to do is read *The Ponder Heart*, for God's sake. All you need to do is read "The Equilibrists" or "Bells for John Whiteside's Daughter" or "Directive" or "The Rocking-Horse Winner."

If you want to write something go back to your real desire and write a short story or poem of your own. I would like to sentence every deconstructionist I know to write ten short stories, twenty poems, and a novel. By the time they were finished they would know the secret. The work of art is its own true thing. It is finished. It is sealed. It came from the artist but not of the artist. Once it is fully imagined it no longer belongs to the psyche that brought it into being. It exists to witness to the mystery of all human experience. It is a study in existence.

The good thing about deconstructionism is that it will remain an acquired taste among a few people who come from the set of good people who keep literature alive by teaching it. God bless them every one. Every time I hear them start deconstructing something it reminds me to get out the book and read the real thing. I do that and am healed from whatever wrecking hammer they had put in my brain.

What next in a finite world? "We're walking along in the changing time," as old Doc said in "The Wide Net." "Everything just before it changes seems to be made of gold."

Learning to Teach

THERE IS NOTHING in the world more satisfying than giving advice and having someone take it. There is nothing that gives me more pleasure than introducing students to pieces of literature that I love, stories and novels and poems that are as much a part of my life as my childhood memories. At Vanderbilt I learned to love Shakespeare. At Millsaps College I was introduced to modern poetry by Doctor George Boyd and to William Faulkner by Eudora Welty.

How could I live without "Petition" by W. H. Auden? ("Publish each healer that in city lives/Or country houses at the end of drives;/. . . look shining at/New styles of architecture, a change of heart.") How could I live without *Go Down, Moses*? Or *The Town, The Hamlet,* and *The Mansion*?

I feel a "holy hush of ancient sacrifice," as Wallace Stevens wrote in "Sunday Morning," when I offer these works of genius to my students. Faulkner speaks to them as he did to me. Many of them are from the rural South. He says to them as he said to me, you are not alone, this is our common heritage, we are driven and beautiful, we plot and fall in love and strive for goodness, we trust our kin and are haunted and sustained by the past, we die and new people take our places in the sun.

I would like to think that I am teaching but really I am just passing the baton. I give them books to read and every week I have them write for thirty minutes about what they have read. It's not a test, just an open-book, in-class writing assignment with a list of ideas and questions I give them. They write dazzling answers to the questions. They make moral judgments and chastise themselves for being judgmental, they see their own grandmothers in Ursúla Buendia and tell their own family histories in answer to Faulkner's stories.

I had worried that reading was going out of style in the United States. I was wrong. Over and over students tell me they "can't wait to get out of school so I'll have time to read." All I am doing is opening some doors. I am dazzled and honored to get to do it.

The War with the Squirrels

AT SEVEN THIS MORNING I spoke to my oldest son on the telephone. It has been forty-seven years since they rolled me into an operating room and cut me open and lifted him from my body. Now he is in Copenhagen, Denmark, with his second wife and their three children and I almost never get to see him or hold him in my arms or touch his face and hair. Motherhood is a strange and powerful thing. I grew this man inside my womb and sent him out into the world. He has given me eight grandchildren, immortality for another hundred years. It seems a great gift. I know how to receive gifts. I am good at being grateful.

I am writing this on a legal pad with a pencil one of my granddaughters brought me from the championships at Wimbledon in the year 2002. She is five years old and is always giving me pencils because she knows I am a writer.

It is fall. This is the time of year when I play a constant and demanding game with the squirrels who live near my hickory trees. Squirrels are addicted to the smell and taste of hickory nuts. They will pass up shelled pecans to crack open the hard green shells of immature hickory nuts. They like to sharpen their teeth on the shells and as soon as the nuts get scarce they begin to chew on the trim of my house. My house is made of California redwood. They have done thousands of dollars worth of damage to the trim over the years. I have spent another thousand having them trapped and taken away by an old fish-and-game man who is an ace at trapping animals. He takes them off in his truck and turns them loose in the woods near a pecan grove.

Lately I am trying another, more exciting, less expensive track with my squirrel problem. I go out on my porch five or six times a day and pick up all the hickory nuts near the house and throw them out into the yard to a stand of cherry trees. I am trying to trick the squirrels into thinking that cherry trees are the nirvana of hickory smell and taste, not my house and porch. Sometimes I hire a twelve-year-old Little League pitcher who lives next door to do the throwing. He is able to pitch the nuts all the way to the vacant lot behind my house where there are maple and oak trees. I do not know if any of this is working but it's a lot of fun to watch John Tucker McCormick throw the nuts so far. I remember when he was inside his mother's stomach and I was helping choose a name for him.

Now he is so tall and strong he could probably throw those hickory nuts a mile if he really tried.

What a wonderful world. I love it here.

OCTOBER 2003

What They Write About

IT IS SUNDAY MORNING. Ever since yesterday afternoon I have been sad because I talked to my five-year-old granddaughter and she said her mother said I should not have bought new clothes for her when she was visiting me last weekend because she didn't need any new clothes. "Here is just what she said," Juliet continued. "She said I have a hundred clothes and I did not need any more."

Juliet is in the middle of her parents' terrible divorce. She spends the weekends with my son and the weeks around the corner with her mother. She is a very wise, self-protective little girl and extremely honest and open. She tells everyone everything that anyone says. (She might make a good writer.) She does not prevaricate or soften the messages or leave out the implied guilt trips. If you don't ask her questions you don't have to hear things, but if you question her you get straight answers.

I am often saddened by things she tells me but in the end I am happy to know that she is so aware and smart and attentive and such a great little politician. (She might make a good president.)

She tests in the extremely high gifted and talented range and goes to a school that teaches in French half of each day. Her mother is English and Juliet has flown back and forth across the Atlantic Ocean dozens of times in her five years. She has visited England, France, Turkey, Tunisia, and several other countries and is exposed to a constant stream of visitors from other cultures. I am in awe of Juliet and am going to learn to do two things. One, stop buying her clothes when she visits me. Two, stop asking her questions unless I really want to hear the answers.

There are deep and powerful emotions surrounding this divorce and I am knee deep in them as I have been since the first child of the misalliance was in the womb. I love these two little red-headed girls with all my heart. I am in constant fear that my son will lose them in some way. No matter how hard I try to stay rational I cannot defeat these emotions with rational thought.

Love and marriage and children and broken hearts and disappointments and dreams that don't come true are the stuff of poetry and fiction. My students know this better than I do. I used to know it, but I have forgotten it because it doesn't affect me as much as it used to, except for grandchildren-in-the-grips-of-divorce sort of problems.

I may be able to write better than my students can but they are closer to the material out of which real stories come into being. I am dazzled by the emotions my students struggle with and write about.

Some of them are learning to use these struggles as material. I am learning how much I have forgotten and left behind.

I am doing the best I can to teach them but there is really very little to teach about writing. All I can do is edit their work to make the writing more beautiful and seductive, and tell them over and over again the few, simple strategies I know. I learned most of them from a book by Ernest Hemingway that I assign to students every semester. It is called *On Writing*. It is a very small book of all the things about writing scattered around in Hemingway's body of work. *On Writing* was put together by the man who is now the editor in chief of Little, Brown, my publisher for many years. An editor at Random House actually made the book but Mike Petsch did the legwork and searched the Hemingway books for the pieces.

It was in that book that I learned to quit each day while I still knew what to write next. I learned to be satisfied by four pages of good, well-written prose and then go out and live my real life and be fresh when I come back to the piece the next morning. I learned to go back frequently and reread the entire story or book up to the place where I was working. And many more things. I cannot recommend this book enough to young writers.

As a teacher I keep telling my students the same things over and over. The ones who are listening and take my advice turn out to be the ones who publish and win prizes. I do not know exactly what role I play in all this but I am having a good time thinking part of the credit goes to me. I love this deal. The students do the hard, mind-wrenching work and all I do is get dressed up in new clothes I buy with my salary and go into the work-room and tell them what to do next. I have arrived at a management position. How wonderful, how unexpected, how divine. My old engineer daddy would adore it. I hope there is a heaven and that he is looking down on me and thinking how well I have turned out.

APRIL 2004

Part Three: Teaching

Teaching, A Journal

"WHAT AM I SUPPOSED TO DO?" I asked Jim Whitehead, when I agreed to teach the graduate fiction workshop in the fall of the year 2000. I had blithely agreed to teach it; then, a week before school began, I panicked and ran to Jim for advice. He founded the creative writing program and nursed it for thirty-four years. Now he was retired but still available for advice.

"Be a coach," he told me. I liked that answer. I was raised by an athlete and spent my youth listening to lectures on playing to win. My own sport was tennis so the best things I know are slanted toward singles tennis.

Here is what it says over the desk where I write.

> Play to win
> First serve advantage
> Never let them see you sweat
> Take care of business
> Slow down
> Stay calm
> Send a message
> Don't let up

No fears

Practice, practice, practice. Matches are won on the practice court

Andre Agassi runs up hills on Christmas Day to get ready for the FIFTH SET AT WIMBLEDON

Stretch the lead. Once Steffi starts winning you cannot stop her

Move your feet

Get in position

Focus

Get your racket back

Keep your eye on the ball

SERVE THE WHOLE

Teaching, A Journal
(Continued)

IN THE FALL of the year 2000 the University of Arkansas hired me to teach two classes in their writing program. I was thrilled with the assignment. I had never taught school but I loved schools and classes and I believed I was ready.

That first fall semester went well. It was easier than I had imagined it would be. The students were bright and well read. I liked them and quickly became maternal, especially about the brightest ones.

I protected myself from my deepest worries by writing them a letter which I passed out in the first class to both my groups. In it I asked them not to come to class with a fresh cold and not to write the details of childhood abuse as I was incapable of reading such details. I remembered two terrible accounts of abuse that I had read in newspapers over the years and which I could not get out of my head. I had expended a great deal of energy burying those accounts and didn't want to add others to their store. One of the things I have never been able to get out of my head was an episode that

Geraldine Ferraro encountered when she was a prosecutor. I am sorry she passed the knowledge on to me and hope she has been able to forget it herself.

So, shielded by my letter, I watched the first semester pass uneventfully and signed on to teach again the next fall.

That second fall is here and already I am feeling vulnerable. I encouraged my undergraduate fiction workshop to such an extent that last week, at the second class meeting, they handed me nine short stories to put on the worksheet. I was elated and proud and clutched their offerings to my chest. The next morning I went to the office to have the secretaries turn the stories into a worksheet for the following Thursday.

As I was removing the paper clips and staples from the stories and putting them in order my eye fell on the first page of a story. A three-year-old girl was being ordered by her father to put on her robe and slippers. THEY WERE IN HER BEDROOM.

I panicked. I hid the story at the end of the stack of stories and hastily prepared the papers for the secretary. I couldn't wait to get the papers out of my possession. I ran from the building and got into my car and drove home. I had forgotten to write a letter to them this second year telling them that I couldn't read that stuff.

I had a bad night. But in the morning I put on my workout clothes and decided I was strong enough to face it. I'll go to the university and get a copy of the worksheet, I decided. Then I'll go to the health club and get on the treadmill and read the damn thing. I am strong. I am brave. I can do it. I'll read it as quickly as I can and make some notes and forget it. If I don't go on and read it I'll think about it all week.

The workshop only meets one night a week and I had five days to go. I had to bite the bullet. I had to soldier on. I had agreed to teach this class and I had to teach it. I was sixty-six years old and no one had ever abused me. I could take it. I could overpower my imagination with my reason. Maybe.

It was Saturday morning and the health club was surrounded by a sea of policemen and yellow tape. The club was having its annual Kids Triathlon. Beautiful, wonderful, marvelous, divine little girls and boys were everywhere, in the pool, on their bikes, on the footpaths. Parents wearing official red shirts were writing down times and calling out warnings at the corners where the bikers had to take sharp turns. At least a hundred children were being adored and loved and fed potassium-laced drinks and health bars that contained more calories than most of the children in the world consume in a week.

I was in the land of plenty with lucky children who are loved. I could do it. I could go inside and read the story. I saw the owner of the club near the bicycle stand, went to her and confided my situation. "Come find me on the treadmill," I told her. "See if I'm strong enough to do this."

"I wouldn't be," she said. She's one of my best friends. She knows how I feel about children. She knows I have twelve grandchildren.

"I'll come check on you when I can," she added and gave me a hug and I went into the building and up the stairs and got a reading rack and climbed on a treadmill and put on my reading glasses and stuck the worksheet on the rack and turned the treadmill up to three point eight with an incline of five and started reading.

IT WASN'T ABOUT CHILD ABUSE. Au contraire. It was about a father making a three-year-old girl put on her robe and slippers and go out into the front yard and look up at her bedroom window so she could see that people could see into her room at night, so she should close the blinds or wear her robe.

The young author thought this was a really mean thing that her father had done to her and probably accounted for her recent breakup with a controlling boyfriend.

Jesus.

Later, after I had done four miles on the treadmill and gone downstairs to watch the leaders come in from the twelve-year-old bicycle leg of the triathlon and gone home and eaten a huge breakfast, I got into the shower. While I was rubbing blonde conditioner on my hair I had an epiphany. I'm going to make a list of stories I want them to write to complement the ones they give me, I decided.

"I'm Glad She Divorced Him"

"It Was Nice of Them to Care What Happened to Me"

"She Tricked Him into Marrying Her So What Did She Expect?"

"My Mother-in-Law Was Only Trying to Help"

"People Are Doing the Best They Can Based on the Information They Have Available at the Moment"

"We Had a Constant Food Supply and a Warm House But We Sure Weren't Satisfied With That"

"I Just Wanted to Protect You From Strangers"

FALL 2001

My Third Year

CLASSES HAVE BEEN GOING on for three weeks. I am learning their names and beginning to hear their stories. No wonder no one gets any writing done after they start teaching. The wonder and responsibility of the lives of young people. My students range in age from eighteen to past thirty. They are wonderful and I am beginning to love them.

I wake at four-thirty in the morning worrying about their lives. The boy who drinks too much and takes drugs, the girl who writes like an early Gwen Head, I overedited one of her poems, I have to fix that tomorrow. How? My favorite student, a six-foot, six-inch-tall genius who was my favorite undergraduate for two years and now is in the MFA program writing fiction and poetry. He is awaiting the birth of his second child. The moon is full, the due date was yesterday, they live in a cabin twenty miles from town, and they are going to deliver the baby themselves with only a nurse-midwife and a babysitter for the three-year-old to help. He delivered the first child, his father is a psychoanalyst and a physician, he says he can do it, the baby is in position,

I am a nervous wreck over this. He has school insurance which would pay for the baby to be delivered in a hospital. Why do I think this is my responsibility? I wish I knew how to pray; still, I think that all will go well. He is a genius and his wife is almost as smart as he is.

What else? Last week a tree fell on one of my undergraduates, a twenty-one-year-old girl who is five months pregnant with her first child. She and her husband were out camping in the woods in a tent. We have had a very dry summer and perhaps that is why a large tree fell in the middle of the night and pinned her to the ground. Her young husband screamed for help. Some campers who were nearby came to help. It took four men to lift the tree from her body. A medivac helicopter managed to land nearby and took her to the hospital. The baby is fine. She is scratched and has cuts on her head and face but was well enough to come to school on Monday and talk to her professors and make arrangements to study at home for the next week or so. My favorite student is delivering his second child in a cabin twenty miles from town!!! A tree fell on one of my undergraduates. Jake is drinking again and didn't come to workshop. One of the professors in the department is depressed and won't take his medication. Another has cancer. Our director is taking a leave of absence in the spring and leaving the graduate theses to Skip Hays and me. I overedited the undergraduates' poetry last week. What do I think I'm doing? I am going to spend the morning writing a short story. I need refuge from all this reality.

I am going to try to remember how to pray. I'm reading V. S. Naipaul's correspondence with his father. It is so lovely. The deep love that passed between these two men is a joy to share. It is easy to see why the younger Naipaul became the great writer that he is. The nurturing letters from his overworked journalist father break my heart and fill me with a desire to be that sort of presence in my students' lives—if not all of them, at least the ones with the talent and drive and will to write.

SEPTEMBER 2002

Worrying

IN THE BEGINNING I was all hope and ego. What others had failed to do I would do. I would be generous, gracious, I would take their stories and make them better, I would be a great teacher and a great coach and a fabulous, unforgettable editor. I would not try to turn their stories into my own. I would let their own voices run down the wide unfolding paths of their imaginations. I would unleash their genius, give them hope, teach them to be professionals. Most of all I would not be jealous of them.

Alas, there was nothing to be jealous of. As the months rolled on into November and Thanksgiving came and we all caught colds from one another, as our heads filled up with fluid and presidential politics invaded literature and took our brains away, I began to lose hope that the teacher evaluations would say BEST TEACHER I EVER HAD. I LOVE HER. HIRE HER AGAIN. WE CAN'T STAND TO LET HER GO.

Miss Popularity in the creative writing staff of the Master of Fine Arts program at the University of Arkansas. Was that what I had been going for?

There had been bright spots. Getting paid was nice. Talking about the students with other professors was fun, especially at the beginning when I thought things were going to start happening, when I believed the talented ones were going to break loose and write stories that would win contests. (Two years later they did. I didn't know how long it was going to take.)

There were other bright spots. If I have one thing to teach it is perseverance and hard work. I love to work. I love to write and I like to rewrite and I don't care how long it takes to get something right. I like to sit down at a typewriter every morning and make something out of nothing. I can take it when half of what I write is not "any good," i.e., publishable. I learn from writing. I feel good after I have been writing and I miss it like crazy when I don't do it.

At least one of the students actually began to believe what I said about writing every day and getting the work done. At the end of the semester she turned in two long stories and showed another one to one of the other teachers. That was the only time I got jealous of anything they did. I wondered why she didn't show them *all* to me.

Also, when I would look around the table during workshop I fancied I saw recognition of the intelligence of what I was trying to teach them in some of their faces. They were believing it even though they weren't all ready to do it yet.

I preached to them that WRITING IS REWRIT-ING. I kept writing that on the blackboard as a joke. "Wait a minute," I would exclaim in the middle of some entirely different matter. "I just thought of something." Then I would run excitedly to the blackboard and write WRITING IS REWRITING.

Another bright spot was a quiet young woman who turned in simple, hopeful stories that were easy to edit and who listened when I told her how to fix them. One of the stories was chosen to go to *Intro*, a publication of the Association of Writers and Writing Programs, which is a very nice coup for a young writer in one of the programs and sometimes even gains them notice from a publisher.

I held on to the hope that they were learning what I was teaching them whether it showed in their stories yet or not. Most of them had been in many writing classes before and knew all the mantras about point of view and so forth. I couldn't help remembering that William Shakespeare and William Faulkner and Anton Chekhov and Cervantes and Turgenev never went to writing classes or sat in workshops letting fourteen other people pick their creations into pieces.

I tried to control the criticism and never let it go past the point where it might be helpful but I'm not sure I succeeded in that. After a few months I fell into the workshop mentality and stopped being careful enough with what I let happen.

Also, I began to worry about how I would grade them. Because they had all had so many writing classes they were very good critics and editors of each other's stories. They could pick stories apart with the best of them. They could talk critically about what was wrong with the stories better than I could because I had tried my best for twenty years to never read criticism or think of writing in the abstract. My modus operandi was just to read the best and most beautiful writing I could find and never read a line of bad writing if I could help it.

But, as I said, I was getting paid so I read their stories with the best attention I could give them.

At the very end of the semester we had a visiting writer. He was not a man whose writing I admired or could even force myself to read so I was dreading having to drive him around for four days. I have always been very careful not to have writer friends unless they are people whose work I really admire. I had asked Larry McMurtry to be our guest but he said he no longer gave advice to people. Then I asked a writer who I thought was a good technician if not a great writer but he didn't want to do the huge amount of work required by the gig. For seven thousand dollars we needed someone to come to town, stay four days and have individual meetings with each of fifteen writers, plus give a public reading and attend my workshop. That's a lot of work for seven thousand dollars in today's creative writing gig market and you get what you pay for as my father knew.

I spent a sleepless night the night before our visiting writer arrived trying to get myself up for entertaining him. I told myself his job was to talk to the students and give them a different perspective on their writings and I should be glad to have the help. I told myself that I would be nice to him and try to remember how weird it is to be in his position. I have been in that position although no amount of money would ever tempt me to read student papers back then.

I tried not to resent the fact that besides being a writer whose work I thought was boring he was the new editor of an anthology and had removed one of my short stories from the new edition. Plus he had published his own story in the book so that was another thing I resented.

RESENTED. Had one semester of teaching creative writing turned me into a RESENTER. Jesus Christ, I muttered. Let me out of here.

The visiting writer arrived. He was a sweet, kind, ex-alcoholic who is part of the large group of teacher-writers who run the writing programs around the United States and invite each other to lecture and seem to believe in what they are doing and work hard to do it well. He had been invited by another faculty member after I couldn't find anyone I admired to accept the job. I should have been grateful that I had anyone to do the work but I kept thinking about the terrible writers who were brought in when I was a student and how cynical it made me when my professors pretended to admire their work. On top of resentment I was getting cynical. No wonder people stop writing when they start teaching, I decided, which dug my resentment grave deeper.

My visitor had been on the wagon for a year. As soon as he arrived he fell off the wagon and started getting drunk every night with an emeritus professor he knew from his past. He met with the students, drank with some of them at lunch and with many of them at night, gave an embarrassing reading, was too hung over to stay at my workshop and told all the students they were wonderful writers.

They loved him. I gave him his check for seven thousand dollars and put him on the plane back to California. So it goes.

The best thing about his visit was knowing *I* didn't have to have a visiting professor again for several years. I knew one thing for sure. Whoever I invite will be a sober person who would not go out and drink with my students. I am the Carrie Nation of the creative writing program and I intend to stay that way.

Meanwhile, onward. I still believe that I am doing more good than harm.

Postscript

At least three of the students I had that fall are well on their way to careers as writers. Two of them have a good agent I found for them. One of them won the Playboy College Fiction Contest. Another sold two stories at once to the *Atlantic Monthly*. The third has sold seven pieces of creative nonfiction and has an assignment from *Outside* magazine for an eighth.

Plus, several of my nonfiction students are selling pieces to good magazines.

It is all taking longer than I thought it would take but it is beginning to happen. I am looking forward to next fall. Who knows what will happen next. This is turning out to be a very exciting thing to do. I think I'm hooked although I still wouldn't do it for free.

Students

THE SECOND YEAR I taught, one of my favorite students was a young woman who was a policewoman for the university. She had a fabulous uniform and a gun. Several times she wore the whole gig to come and see me in my office, but only once did she consent to wear it to class. "Packing," the admiring male students said that day. "She's packing."

It took only a little nudging on my part to get her to begin writing about her experiences on the university police force. The other students loved reading her papers, especially in the nonfiction class. She was taking both my graduate nonfiction workshop and my undergraduate fiction workshop. She was a wonderful student because she believed what I told her and was willing to try the things I suggested. After she began to write about her police experiences she quickly saw how it could become a book of essays. By the end of the semester she had quit her job and gone to work in the bookstore instead. She had seen that in order to write the truth about the police force she would have to leave it.

The last day she worked for the campus police she came to my office wearing her complete uniform and her LOADED GUN and brought me roses for my desk. What a charming girl! What a wonderful way to end the semester.

I have no doubt that sooner or later she is going to write the book of essays and that it will be published. I can't think of anything more refreshing than a look at a campus police department through the eyes of a young female officer.

She had stories about special treatment for athletes, drunken students at ball games, drunken alumni screaming to have their confiscated liquor back, corruption in the department, all sorts of inside information that she feared would get her sued or fired. I told her to write the stories and we'd decide later what she could publish. Instead she quit the job. Good choice, as my psychiatrist used to say.

APRIL 2002

The Ice Storm

I TOLD THE STUDENTS we had to leave the building before dark because ice was on the streets but they said, no, it was almost the last class and we had to workshop all the essays. Okay, I said, then we have to figure out a way to take each other home. How far away are your cars from the building because the parking lot is a sheet of ice? The fat, dependable girl said, mine is near the journalism department. The thin New Yorker said, I can take two people wherever they need to go.

They talked among themselves and got it worked out while I pretended to be engrossed in the next paper on the worksheet. I had begun the semester full of hope and ambition for their work but my interest was waning now that it was December. There is no substitute for talent. All the hard work in the world doesn't make up for not having the poetic tools to make what you write seductive. I had hoped to make one or two of these students into writers but the muse was somewhere else this semester.

This was a creative nonfiction workshop. It wasn't as heady and charged as a fiction workshop but in the end the same thing was happening. The most interesting things they wrote were small, autobiographical asides in their researched pieces. In a piece about being an army brat a thin, yoga-expert girl threw in a line about being forced to join and conduct prayer services before cheerleading sessions in a small, Georgia town. I told her to make a short story out of the material. "It was my day to lead the prayer service and I was terrified," should be the lead, I told her. These were words out of her mouth when the class asked her to talk more about the incident. The story had a natural ending. She was saved from having to lead the prayers because the coach had discovered a girl necking in an automobile at a football game and had the cheerleaders do a therapy session for the errant girl instead of having their usual prayers. The cheerleaders formed a circle around the bad girl and prayed for her until she cried and repented.

On the afternoon of the ice storm the students worked very hard and the class lasted three hours and forty minutes instead of the usual three. When it was over we all went down together to the parking lot and got into the cars that were near the building. By the time the class ended I was back into an optimistic mood about their work. They were learning, they were working, it takes time, the muse will come if she is summoned.

While we were waiting for a young man to bring his car across the parking lot I overheard a conversation and it reminded me of what it's really like to be a student and what they mostly, really are driven to think about.

"Celia Markham wants to go out with you," the tall, gangly genius told the tall, good-looking boy with money who actually had talent although he wouldn't use it.

"I don't want to go out with her," he answered. "But I'd go out with that yoga girl."

"Celia only wants to fuck you," the genius added.

"I'd fuck her," the good-looking boy agreed.

"That's all she wants," the genius said. "Meet us down at Baby Lee's. We'll be there in twenty minutes."

Well, I decided, this class is definitely not a waste of time. I got into my car and drove home, remembering when I was a graduate student and used to go out after a Joyce seminar with a student from Montana. One night, after we had been studying the Molly Bloom episode, I made love to him in an eighteenth-century graveyard on top of a hill near the campus. We were laughing the whole time. I tried hard to remember what it was like to be young and wild and full of juice but I couldn't remember. What the hell, I decided, I'm going to give them all A's like Eudora Welty did when she taught us.

Creative Nonfiction
(as Fiction)

WE HAD A WAR and an ice storm and still they kept
on writing. What does that tell you about ego and
ambition? Not that writing was the only thing going on
in my undergraduate creative writing workshop which
met on Wednesday nights in Kimpel Hall on the campus of the University of Arkansas where I work now
that I can't think of anything else to write.

There were twelve students in the class, a one-eyed
veteran of the Vietnam War, three chubby girls with pretty
faces, a thin girl whose name I never could remember,
a wealthy divorcée from Little Rock, and six tall young
men, all sexy, interesting, and talented. Three of the
young men were friends before the class began. They
were the editors of the campus literary magazine, which
had recently been given a large sum of money by the
Tyson Foundation and was gearing up to publish a 150-
page special edition in the spring.

Listen, any one of the young men in that class would
have kept young women coming to class when I was
in college, much less six of them. Plus, the one-eyed

veteran wasn't bad-looking either and after he started turning in work and the other students read it, I noticed the divorcée moved her chair next to his and kept it there. Talent has its uses.

We had two classes before September 11. On the first class after that I expected them to be unprepared and to want to talk about the attack on New York City and Washington, D.C., but they surprised me by coming to class having read the assignments and ready for business. We were reading Turgenev and Chekhov while I waited for them to begin turning in stories to put on the worksheet but again they surprised me by turning in stories almost immediately. Most of the students were from rural or small-town backgrounds and I had thought Turgenev would be good for them and it had turned out to be true. They understood landlords because of the big corporations which run northwest Arkansas and they especially understood kindly landlords, what with the hundred-thousand-dollar grant to the literary magazine and so forth.

So they wrote on through the war on terrorism without a hitch, turning in stories about children who blow up pigs by mistake, children who kill their father's fighting cocks to stop him from drinking, children who manipulate their parents to get candy, children who don't answer their parents' phone calls after they get to college, children who don't visit the nursing home enough and feel guilty afterwards, children who meet

Jesus in a meadow and ask him to bring their dead father back to life, children who grow up and take dope and then quit and go back to being sober.

It was several weeks before anyone began to write about the war. It was the veteran who wrote about it. He started putting doomed passengers into his stories. They were always about to get on the fated airplanes when his love stories ended. No matter how much the other students begged him to stop putting doomed airline passengers into his stories he kept on doing it right up to the last class of the semester. It was his signature plot move. He wouldn't budge on it.

Meanwhile the real action was taking place between one of the chubby girls and an editor of the literary magazine and the thin girl whose name I couldn't remember because she seldom came to class.

The chubby girl wanted to date the editor and was losing about three pounds a week to gain her objective. She wasn't that chubby to begin with and by October she was looking like a contender. The thin girl was still sitting by him but I noticed he was referring questions to the chubby girl.

A redheaded girl meanwhile was going out for coffee after class with the even taller and more handsome second-in-command at the magazine and he asked her out loud in class to submit her work to the magazine for publication. The four of them left together after every class as the fall wore on into November. Then the ice storm came and power went out for four days and no one could print or write no matter how much I had preached to them about writing first drafts by hand and even went over to the campus bookstore and bought some legal pads and gave them to students for a joke.

FALL 2001

The Semester from Hell

IT WAS MY THIRD SEMESTER teaching creative writing at the University of Arkansas and I had decided to tell the graduate students the truth about what they were writing. I had the idea in my head that I should be a take-no-prisoners coach and demand from them the things I demand from myself when I am writing, absolute devotion, contempt for bad writing, the ability to go back into a piece as many times as it takes to make it lush and beautiful and true.

So, instead of writing pleasant little queries in the margins of their stories, I did what I do to my own first drafts. I marked out words that ruined the sound. I marked out whole sections that were unnecessary or preachy or poorly written. I wrote NO in the margin when I came to something that was really bad writing or written for its shock value or just ugly or boring.

Reading the stories that were turned in to my workshop for the first three weeks was torture for me. They were so bad, with a few exceptions, that I thought every day about resigning my position, quitting, giving up. But in a few weeks the younger writers began to improve.

Because I had rejected their first manuscripts and refused to pretend to take them seriously, they actually began to write stories that were better than the first ones. A few of them even used my tortured editing to improve their stories. Then, suddenly, a breakthrough. A young man from Louisiana turned in a story so fine and polished I told him to send it immediately to good magazines, beginning with the *Atlantic Monthly*.

A few weeks later it was accepted, along with a second story, for publication in the *Atlantic*. This stirred up jealousy in some of the other graduate students but the ones with real talent were encouraged by their fellow student's success.

By the end of the semester his closest friend had won the Playboy College Fiction Contest for 2002. I took more pleasure from the success of those two young writers than I have taken from my own successes in many years.

I am beginning to understand why people love to teach. It is challenging and terrifying and uncertain. Then, suddenly something you have said or done makes a real difference in a student's life and you are so proud and happy.

I must remember not to expect this to happen every day or even every year. And I must not forget this joy or be too greedy for more of it.

FALL 2002

Drunks, Dope Addicts, and Losers, Characters My Students Give Me

IT IS NOVEMBER and I am tired of teaching these sad students. They are like baby birds waiting to be fed. They are older than the leaders of the Lewis and Clark expedition and they look like I have been beating them when I tell them the truth about their writing and tell them I am not going to give them A's for turning in first drafts and expecting me to edit and revise their stories.

I do not like them anymore. The semester, which started out so full of hope, is running down and, with the exception of two very talented young men, nothing is happening in my workshop of which I can be proud. I'm not teaching and they're not learning. I cannot line edit first drafts about dope addicts, drunks, or losers.

In an attempt to jump-start the remainder of the semester I wrote them the following letters.

Dear Students,
You have to know things to be a writer. You have to read constantly and broadly and be curious and "continually roaming with a roving eye."

If you are not writing well and happily, or if you feel your writing is forced, stop for a while and read or go out into the world and watch building projects or street-repair crews or get a job in a mall for Christmas or get into the car and drive to a city and look at art. Learn, learn, learn, be curious, and, if possible, uncritical. Everywhere men and women are doing wonderful things, marvelous things, interesting things. Write paragraphs about what you see and don't try to turn them into anything but praise and understanding.

If you are teaching, find out the life stories of your students and write little sketches of them to use later. Ask them who their grandparents were and how they came to live in the places where they lived.

Learn, learn, learn, read, read, read. I will be thinking about you and wishing you well every day.

Ellen

Second letter

Dear Students,

I am enjoying teaching you and getting to know you *all*. Each one of you has talent and the ability to write and publish if you also have the will and stamina to do that difficult thing.

A few of you, maybe three or four, are making A's in my workshop so far and that worries me deeply. I want to give you all A's. As I told you at the beginning of this class to make an A you have to participate well in the class discussions and you are *all* doing that, and you have to write three stories *or* two stories and a brilliant rewrite of one of them.

In other words you have to give me at least one finished, rewritten story by the end of class that I would put into a magazine if I were editing that magazine.

I can't give you an A for turning in first drafts and not working hard to make them better. If you are seriously blocked and can't turn in good, finished work to me before the semester ends, please call me and we will set up a time when we can talk.

We are going to be very busy from November 17 to November 20. The next week I will be gone. The week after Thanksgiving we will begin our final push to the end of the semester. Talk to me *now* if you are having trouble writing a story that will earn you an A in this class.

With all good wishes and good luck for your work.
　　　Ellen

Postscript

Here is the hard part of this letter. Please read this carefully. I have to tell you this. What you do with the information is up to you.

If you are writing sad, dark stories about drunks or dope addicts and if the characters in these stories are not attractive in any way or redeemed by hope or charity or goodness of any kind, if the settings for the stories are bars, if the characters are losers, then you won't publish these stories anywhere except in small, unstable literary magazines that don't pay enough to make up for the postage. Publishers are business people. They are in business to sell books. The few people left in the United States who buy books are not drunks or dope addicts and don't want to read about such things.

Just because you see such stories in magazines doesn't mean that the writers are making a living writing.

Go back into your lives and find the places that were charged by hope, goodness, charity, joy, intelligence, love, courage, understanding, learning, and write about those moments.

Ellen

At our class meeting after I put the second letter in their university mailboxes they came to class in a very subdued state. A couple of them had fresh haircuts and were dressed in shirts and ties. It was a serious class. I didn't ask them if they had gotten the letter and they didn't mention it.

Meanwhile I had taken a story on which I had written "this isn't worth your talent," and thrown it away. I got a fresh copy of it and wrote on the top, "This is almost finished. You can start on something else."

I may not last long at this teaching career. I certainly won't last long if I have to teach the graduate fiction workshop very often. The next time I am scheduled to teach it will be in the spring of 2004. It will be the second semester and one of my confederates in this dream merchant scam will have had the students first and, I hope, made some dent in their needfulness and disorder.

It's a paycheck, I tell myself. And I will tell them the truth no matter what happens or whether they like it or not.

FALL 2002

How Can I Help These Students Learn to Write?

I HAVE TO LOVE THEM. I have to believe that they each have a story to tell and can learn to tell it in their true voices. I have to be brutally honest and kind at the same time.

I have to teach them to write a line of poetry. Then a second line. And a third. And a fourth and so on.

I have to find the poetry within their first drafts and say, here is the good line. Believe in this line.

I need to find a way to grade them, but, so far, after three years, the best I can do is give A's to anyone who really tries and turns in the requisite number of manuscripts or tells me enough sad stories about funerals they have attended.

As I begin my fourth year of teaching I will do better. Creative writing classes should not really be graded but since it has to be done I want to devise a system that makes some sort of sustained sense. The one I have been using isn't dependable in a changing world. We have had ice storms, flu epidemics, and a war while I was teaching. These things are real barriers to finishing creative work and since I experience that in my own work I believe the students' excuses too readily.

I picked up a book of essays about teaching on a sales table at Barnes and Noble and began to randomly turn the pages. One woman said that she had given up assigning three stories a semester, which has become the gold standard for writing workshops, and begun to tell the students to turn in five pages a week. She did not say whether these assignments had to lead to a story. This is the question my boss, Molly Giles, asked when I told her I thought this was a fine idea. Molly said she used a version of that method when she taught novel writing. I've decided that is what I will do this coming fall semester when I teach the undergraduate fiction workshop. These are the best writing students in the English department. They have to take creative writing I and creative writing II before they can take the workshop.

I am looking forward to teaching them. I will tell them they can turn in finished stories if they wish or they can turn in five pages of prose a week and if any of these assignments begin to turn into stories or the workshop can help them find ways to expand what they have written to make stories, well and good.

If this works well with the undergraduates I may use the same method when I teach the graduate fiction workshop in the spring. I am learning. I hope.

FALL 2003

Onward

August 1

In a few weeks I will begin my fourth year as a writing teacher. Is it possible to teach verbal skills? No. Is it possible to polish a stone until it becomes a mirror? Maybe.

It is possible to be an editor if the raw material is heartfelt and true. It is possible to be a coach if the players are sober and not on drugs and have drive and ambition and can learn to believe in themselves and will stay home and write instead of staying out on the streets drinking beer and looking for love in all the wrong places.

It may even be possible to keep the untalented students from blaming their failures on me. That is my goal for the coming year.

I have had pleasant surprises in the past three years. I have had housewives publish poems I edited and their joy is all the reward I need. I have had graduate students publish in good magazines and win awards and that gives me joy and hope for the new year.

This fall, the only writing class I will be teaching is the fiction workshop for undergraduates. Many of them are students I have had in other classes and I am looking forward to teaching them again. Maybe some real short stories will come out of the class. Maybe we will have honors, rewards, treasure. Maybe I will be a magician for these handpicked, special students. Maybe I'll get lucky.

Last year I made Buddhist prayer flags to bring luck to my graduate students. I had them write their initials on pieces of blue cotton cloth and then I hung the flags on the icy winter trees. A few weeks later one of them called to say he had won the Playboy College Fiction Contest.

I don't believe in magic but I believe in luck, especially in this business, or art, or whatever it is I tell myself I'm doing, and now, to compound the hubris, teaching.

August 28
The first meeting of the fiction writing class. Leo Van Scyoc, the angel genius who makes the schedules for the Department of English, has given me the beautiful seminar room where the graduate workshops usually meet. This may be to make up for the fact that I have agreed to let extra students into the class. A workshop should not be more than fifteen students and this one will have seventeen. I will manage. Since I don't know what I am doing anyway I suppose I can accommodate seventeen students if I make up my mind to do it.

"And we are here as on a darkling plain/Swept with confused alarms of struggle and flight . . ." These are young minds that I see before me. I will teach them what I know, by God. I am honored to get to do this work, deeply touched to be here.

AUGUST 2003

Hitting a Snag in the Teaching Game

September 2

Second meeting of my undergraduate fiction workshop. A female student is writing horror stories about werewolves that contain so much violence and verbal abuse I can hardly bear to read them. She insists this is all she wants to write and is going to keep on writing it so I called her this morning and told her I thought it would be a good idea for her to drop my class and take one taught by a man we have here this semester who publishes "genre" fiction. That's an academic code name for writing that doesn't aspire to be literature and makes no claim to beauty. This may be a class thing.

I am learning. As soon as I finished talking to the student I called the chairwoman of the English department and told her I was sending the woman to her to see if her schedule could be changed. The chairwoman was marvelously understanding.

This afternoon I have to meet with the young woman and tell her again that the only way she can stay in my class is to write two more stories that are not horror or fantasy stories and which do not contain gratuitous violence. I am treading on eggs here, fragile egos. I want to help the young woman but I don't think she is going to let me help her. I will protect myself in this matter and protect the integrity of the class.

"You should call this class teaching writing literature then," she told me when we had our meeting.

"I took that for granted," I answered. "I assumed anyone would know the Department of English was teaching literature."

What a tangled skein. She dropped the class and I am glad she did. I am learning as I go along. But it isn't easy. I took her down the hall and introduced her to the "genre" writing teacher and she agreed to take his class. But she didn't thank me and she didn't smile. You can't please everyone, I knew when I was young, but had forgotten in the protected world I lived in until I started teaching. I had to deal with reviewers when I was publishing books but at least I didn't have to have them scowling at me in person in the halls.

September 9

I went over to the university yesterday to pick up the *New York Times* and stopped at my office to leave off some papers. On the sidewalk outside the building I ran into the young woman who is writing about werewolves. She was trying not to speak to me but I said hello twice and asked her how the new class was coming along. "I haven't met it yet," she said, and swept by me. I still maintain that it is not my job to read about werewolves killing their young. Then why this strange haunting guilt? I cannot be a psychiatrist to troubled students. It does not fit my personality and disrupts the work I want to do with the other students in the class.

NOTE: We need different books at different times in our lives. When we are young we need poetry and fiction to tell us how to live our lives. Later, we need information so we can be informed members of our culture. If our lives are peaceful we have time to learn anthropology and biology and geology and political science, and all the things we are taught when we are too young and confused emotionally to understand what we are being offered.

As we get older we become wiser, I hope, or at least we must try to be wise.

SEPTEMBER 2003

Rip Van Winkle and the Unwanted Wings

HOW CAN I TEACH my undergraduates to write short stories? In many ways this is the easiest semester I have had since I began teaching. I feel that I know what I am doing and what to expect to a greater extent than I did three years ago but each student and each class present new problems and I feel I must devise new strategies for solving those problems.

The real strategy is to tell them the truth about their work in a kind and helpful manner that does not harm the "dust on the butterfly's wings," as Hemingway called Scott Fitzgerald's talent.

Perhaps one of them has that talent. What a wonderful thing it would be to help someone become a writer who would give the world the gift of an unforgettable story, a story or poem that helps us live our lives and that stays with us for generations.

Like Dylan Thomas's poetry, "The force that through the green fuse drives the flower . . ." Or Salinger's wonderful story "For Esmé—with Love and Squalor," or Chekhov's story "The Student," which he wrote after many years of writing many stories not half so fine, or Faulkner's *Go Down, Moses.*

Such a student with such a gift is not the only dream of my daily work as a teacher. I want to teach each of these students that writing is an easy, natural act. It becomes difficult when the writer tries to push an idea farther than it needs to go or gets writing confused with being rich and famous.

My lovely student, Miroslav Penkov, from Bulgaria, is writing well and clearly in his second language. Sometimes he writes the dialogue in Bulgarian and then translates it into English.

This week he turned in a lovely, very Russian story about an old man who loves only money and power. He has had a succession of mistresses who are all called Megan. He insists they dye their hair golden red to resemble the young Megan who jilted him when he was young and poor.

After many pages of setting up the old man to have to pay for the havoc he has wreaked in the world of business, Miro has wings begin to grow on the old man's back. They are growing exactly two inches a year. In the end the old man has the current Megan cut off the wings, which creates a cascade of health problems that ends with the old man in a wheelchair unable to feed himself or move.

I am tempted to tell Miro that he can achieve all the ends of the story by having the old man simply grow older and become incapacitated by osteoporosis and other health problems. Life can exact its revenge without the help of the supernatural.

Will this take the dust from the butterfly's wings? Will it chastise Miro's creative imagination? I am going to ask him to try it both ways and then decide for himself. As it is, the ending is too contrived but the old Russian writers he likes to read would probably prefer the angel wings.

Fortunately Miro listens to help and criticism better than my American students. He has come from a colder, more dangerous world and doesn't expect things to be easy. I believe I can tell him what I think without harming him.

My other problem this week is a beautiful sorority girl named Amber who had the brainstorm last week to rewrite "Rip Van Winkle" and set it in a contemporary office building. I suggested that she use a quotation from the other "Rip" to begin the story so the reader would not be surprised when Ripp, her character, goes to sleep and wakes to find himself with a long beard in a world he could not have imagined. She was very taken with the idea. Now if I can get her to write about something she knows or somewhere she has been. The most mysterious thing about her story is the office she imagines in Ripp's life before he is transformed. She says it is her father's real office.

Onward. No one said this would be easy but I had imagined it might be or I would never have agreed to try to do it.

FALL 2003

Teaching, A Journal
(Continued)

September 29

I am trying to teach my students that writing is an easy, natural act. Sometimes it is an easy, natural act, then it becomes difficult because the writer tries to take his idea further than it needs to go. Or he doesn't know enough yet to take the idea further. A writer has to know some stuff, he has to study, has to be "continually roaming" with a curious eye, has to be reading, learning, watching, thinking.

Study epistemology, logic, ethics, geology, biochemistry, water tables, visit farms and factories, travel if it's possible, by foot and bicycle and by automobiles and trains. Keep a journal or at least have a pad and pencil with you to write down impressions. Memory will serve for most things, but street names, county names, wonderful names of people, all those things will come in handy someday if you keep on writing.

Another thing that happens to young writers, especially in writing schools, is that they become jealous and competitive. Then writing becomes a contest and the muse disappears. When writing becomes a contest, the simple, earnest desire to communicate wonder or terror or delight or praise gets lost in pride and the delusions of the ego.

How to teach my students to hold on to the simple desire to tell a story or make someone laugh or just tell about something to someone else? I don't know how to make this happen, but since it is my goal, I will find a way if I try. I want to be the best teacher these young people have ever had. Surely my desire to do that will find a way. Water always runs downhill. Osmosis. Perhaps that's how I will make it happen. I'll be there with the knowledge that thirty years of writing and publishing has given me and I'll be as generous with that knowledge as I can and some of it will flow into the students.

I must remember to be kind. It is hard to be criticized, easy to praise. Praise is a muse of sorts. She is a goddess in the realm of human relationships. I will serve her if I can.

Wednesday at dawn, October 1
I have been learning to meditate, or thinking of it and doing it a small amount.

This morning I drank a small coffee, looked at the stars, saw the Big Dipper and the Little Dipper, then hurriedly dressed, am hurriedly writing this and then running out to a Pilates class. Just for fun.

Wednesday at dawn, October 15

A bright, waning moon, like a spotlight, still high in the sky at 5:45 in the morning. The sky is very clear and dark, beautiful, blue. The stars are shining and bright. It's chilly, the first real fall day. It has been two weeks since I wrote in this journal. The leaves have changed color and begun to fall and color the ground. I have been deep into a meditative state, doing breathing exercises, listening to Andrew Weil and Jon Kabat-Zinn on meditation and breathing. I was led to these wonderful CDs by listening over and over again to an old Zen Buddhist tape by Alan Watts. I profited so much from his lectures on Zen that I began to think I should go to the bookstore and see if there were other tapes on the same subject that I could buy to keep me calm for the work I have to do with my students and also the exciting and scary things that go on with my large family. I have become the guru and matriarch of sixteen people, or of some of them, the ones I know well because they live near me.

I have to be strong and mentally alert and objective and all the things my psychiatrists were for me. I have to keep in mind how dear all these people are to me, my family and my students. I have to keep on learning and trying to be wise and clear. I have to learn so I can teach. Here is what has happened since I wrote in this journal two weeks ago. Good things with my students. Hardin came to see me and said he was back at work on his book, perfecting it. It is already written. He is going to get it to my agent, Don Congdon, by November. Josh is being wonderful, very helpful in class. Wolf has cut his education class twice to come early to class. I am cutting him slack because he is writing well and trying so hard, burning the candles at both ends. He has hiked in the Himalaya. He will be all right and I will give him an A for the writing no matter how late he has to be to class.

Leslie has an idea for a book and is hot on the trail of her dream. Steve has a big idea that he got from reading *In Suspect Terrain*. One of my undergraduates wrote a story about his wife, who died accidentally. It was so touching we were all in tears. He looks like he is twenty-one. Yet he has a child and a dead wife. Or else he has an imagination the size of the moon.

So many other stories from my students and my work at the university. Plus, Tulane is asking me to be the Mellon Fellow for a semester. I've never been a Fellow and it would be all right with Molly and Skip if I take the position for one semester.

I am going to Mary Margaret Healy's wedding next week. Into New Orleans to stay at the Windsor Court, have dinner at Antoine's, see the wedding, go to the reception at the Plimsoll Club, then spend Saturday with my darling, darling granddaughters.

I will see Mother on my way back.

I am trying to drink green tea with ginseng instead of coffee. I wish I could talk to my old psychiatrist, Ed White. I might try to do it or to talk to Gunther Perdigao, my first psychiatrist, my Freudian.

SEPTEMBER–OCTOBER 2003

After Six Weeks of Classes

October 2

Things are settling down in my undergraduate fiction workshop. These are the best students in the English department, honors students, creative writing majors, powerful, self-assured, well read, smart. I'm lucky to get to teach them.

Here's what's happening. Remember I told you there were seventeen students in the class. That has shrunk to fifteen, which is about perfect. The tall, very beautiful, blond girl had her heart broken two weeks ago. Her boyfriend of two years threw her over to drink with the Pi Kappa Alphas. She mourned for a week, missed classes, then started going out for coffee and crying on the shoulder of the strongest and most mature of my male students. I had him in fiction readings class last semester and his maturity and usefulness in the class never wavered. Also, he's a good, smart writer and critic. He is not classically handsome but has the kind of quiet male power a girl can lean on. I couldn't have imagined a better man for her at this point. "He's not my boyfriend," she has told me several times. "We're just studying together."

Been there, done that, I should have answered, but I am learning to keep my mouth shut when the students confide in me.

I suppose she is going to break his heart before the semester is over because she really is stunningly beautiful. My wild, creative, six-foot, three-inch writer from the Delta is also hanging out with them so I suppose he's in love with her too. She is a quiet, dignified girl. I think she will help me keep this second young man in line. He is so smart, so imaginative, so energetic it is hard to get him to sit still. He lives at such a fast pace that he always forgets to register for the next semester's classes. This is the second semester that he has come to me at the last minute and begged to be allowed into classes that were already full. I can't resist him. He is straight out of my gene pool. Maybe if I help civilize him someone will be doing the same thing for some of my progeny somewhere in the world. He thinks I am crazy about *him* but it's his mother down in the Delta with whom I feel the deep connection.

He is so talented, such a quick study, so interested in so many things. I let him into a graduate class last year and he paid me back by learning to write. Now he is the best and most generous critic in the seminar.

He's writing a novel based on *On the Road* by Jack Kerouac. Except my student's book is funny and lighthearted and not self-destructive. The other male students say "this reminds me of *On the Road*" and both they and the student author take this as a huge compliment to the manuscript.

I stopped class when we were editing it the other day to declare, "I hate drugs and alcohol and cigarettes and unlawful behavior. I am the Carrie Nation of this writing program. Why would an intelligent person want to do something that makes them dumb." Then I gave them a five-minute sermon about sugar addictions and alcoholism and wasted lives.

The young women were all shaking their heads in agreement. I couldn't read the young men's faces. The ones who agreed with me wouldn't dare admit it to the other men.

"Au contraire!" yelled my gorgeous young man from the Delta. "Strongly disagree."

"I'm calling your mother," I told him. It is a threat I've been giving him for two semesters. I think he wonders if I mean it. I would call her if I didn't think that he was shaping up under the force of his ambition and dreams of glory.

He has captured my imagination. Also, his generous editing of their work has made him popular with everyone in the class. No one minds him showing off or coming roaring into class talking about infinity and saying, WHAT IS REAL AND HOW DO WE KNOW IT?? WHERE ARE WE, AND WHAT ARE WE DOING INSIDE A BUILDING ON A DAY AS BEAUTIFUL AS TODAY?

My most prolific student (shall we call him Matthew) is also turning into an ace line editor. He has learned the power of compression in writing. He believes, as I did when I was writing at my finest, that every word must earn its way. He sits on my left, very near to me, and has sort of declared himself a polished, real writer in the midst of neophytes. He is not as talented as some of the other students but he is making up for it with acquired skills in the trade. I didn't teach him these editing skills. He picked them up in creative writing I and II from my colleague Molly Giles and one of our best graduate students. This young man means a lot to me. He tells me that what we are doing in the writing program works where there is fertile ground. Even though I need the job right now I wouldn't keep on doing it if I thought it was a scam. There have been plenty of times when I thought the whole writing program network around the United States was an elaborate scam to give easy work to unsuccessful writers. Even if that were true, on a scale of one to ten it is about a five for usefulness to the culture.

This young man makes me believe it is at least a seven or an eight.

Update, April

The prolific, hardworking student I called Matthew just won the departmental Fiction Award for Undergraduates. The beautiful girl is going to be a graduate student in the English department. The young man from Bulgaria is in my graduate fiction workshop and is writing wonderful magical stories that dazzle the graduate students. His name is Miro Penkov. He says he cannot write in Bulgaria because there are four fabulous writers there already and no one else can get published. We are telling him he must not believe that is true but we are glad to have him here nonetheless. He has a wonderful scientific mind and is very helpful to other students when they touch on scientific subjects. Plus, he is a perfect student, turning in work on time with no typographical or spelling errors. My native English writers can learn much from Miro.

OCTOBER 2003, APRIL 2004

The Geology Field Trip

October 2

I took my graduate creative nonfiction class on a field trip to see the two-hundred-foot cut through the Boone Formation (a plateau in northwest Arkansas). This was to pay them back for reading *In Suspect Terrain*, by John McPhee. I am beginning to understand that I can't teach them everything at once. I can expose them to some of the things that have been valuable to me as a writer and hope some of them profit from what I know. They don't all need to know the same things. They are not all inspired by the same sort of books or by the same experiences.

I believe in a sound mind in a sound body. More than anything else I want to show them that there is a wide and wonderful and exciting world outside of the creative writing program and its uncertainty and disappointments. There is so much to be seen and learned and explored and written about. They forget that when they spend too much time worrying about their lives or hanging out on Dickson Street drinking beer and waiting to fall in love.

The cut through the Boone Formation was made to build a shopping center containing a T. J. Maxx, a Best Buy, and a Shoe Carnival. It is a marvelous thing to see. The history of the Ozark Plateau going back to the time when this land was an inland sea six or seven hundred miles north of the equator, with a sandy shore somewhere in Kansas. This part of that sea was part of its continental shelf. The limestone and chert of the wall is filled with fossils at the level of the parking lot behind the Shoe Carnival where we were exploring.

Did they learn anything from going to see a wall of ancient earth history? Did it inspire them to read the book with deeper understanding? Was it fun to pretend we were geologists for an afternoon? I don't know. I can only follow my best instincts and hope it was a good idea.

Luckily one of the three undergraduates in the class is a geology student. He is a geology and English major but is mostly interested in geology. Earth Science, he calls it. I call it The Mothership.

His name is Jay Taylor and he is a beautiful, thin, intense young man who carries a book bag full of rocks with him everywhere he goes. He gave me a rock that is more than a billion years old last week. He found it on a real geology field trip to Oklahoma the week before. Also he showed me a large sandstone rock and a bag of ground-up sandstone he got from a quarry near their dig. It is toxic and causes irreparable lung damage if inhaled. He has it in his book bag in a single plastic freezer bag. "Put the sandstone dust away," we advised him, after we had finished exploring the wall and were happily sitting on stools in a local coffee shop having iced sports tea and quiche and banana nut bread.

"I will," he said. "I just keep forgetting to take it out of the bag."

(It weighs five or ten pounds. It is a very large bag of toxic sandstone dust.)

I have a beautiful undergraduate named Rivers who teaches Pilates at the athletic club where I work out every morning. She has to get up at four thirty every morning to be at the club by five. Then she has classes all afternoon, then has a second job in a gift store at a golf course. I don't know how she has time to study. She has been looking tired lately and that bothers me.

Rivers drove with me to the field trip because I had asked her to take photographs with my camera. On top of her other accomplishments she is a gifted photographer. Later that afternoon she left the coffee shop with a young man who is one of the stars of our graduate program. I immediately began to worry. Two beautiful young people thrown together on my watch. What if one of their hearts was broken. Would it be my fault?

October 6

The photographs came back from the field trip. Half of the photographs were of the young man who had taken Rivers home from the coffee shop. He is very handsome and powerful, charismatic and hard to catch. In one photograph he had climbed thirty feet up the vertical rock wall. Rivers had climbed almost as high as he was. I don't know who took the photographs of them together clinging to rocks, daring gravity and each other. Fortunately I had not seen that going on. I was farther down the wall searching for fossils with Wolf and Dusty and Leslie and Marissa.

"Is something going on between these two?" Dusty asked, when I ran into her yesterday and showed her the photographs.

"Oh, God," I said. "I hope not. Is this my fault? They might get hurt."

"They look fine to me," Dusty said. "I saw them both this morning."

October 2003

Postscript

Nothing developed between them except friendship and admiration. Rivers has graduated and is touring Europe with friends. The young man is teaching summer school and waiting for an agent to send his novel to publishers. I would take a vow not to worry so much but I would have to have a prefrontal lobotomy to keep the vow and that seems excessive.

JULY 2004

Monday at Dawn

I STARTED OFF TO GO to a Pilates class at six a.m. at the athletic club, then came back home after half a block of driving. The stars were glorious and there was a small waning moon. A CD of Jon Kabat-Zinn talking about the way we waste our lives rushing from one thing to the next trying to fulfill ambitions or serve obsessions stopped me and I went back home, turned off all the lights in my house and went out on the back porch to view the early morning stars and moon. It would be good to go out in the early morning to finish dying if it's true one has to die.

OCTOBER 2003

The Big Question

HAVE I BEEN TOO HARD on the students in the past? Am I being too nice to them now? All I know for sure is that if I show work to my agent and he says "it isn't working" I lose interest in it. A long time ago, when I was just beginning to publish, my agent or editor would tell me I had to do certain things to make a piece of writing better and I would fiercely go back to work and change the parts they thought were "wrong."

Having a salary and being a professor has changed how I react to that sort of criticism. Half the time I just go on writing the way I was writing without having *any* interest in changing or rewriting the piece. Is this the effect that teaching has on writers? Is this why so many of my most talented friends never published again after they began to teach?

I have written a book of stories, a novel, and a novella in the past year and I don't want to rewrite any of them. I like them as they are. "The characters are just talking," my agent tells me about these pieces of fiction but he has no suggestions as to how I could make the pieces more publishable. Maybe I just *want* to write dialogue. I know the characters I am writing about so well I don't need to describe them or comment on their behavior or conversation so I just amuse myself by telling their stories in dialogue.

I like what I am doing with these stories. I am having a very good time being a writer with no audience. I am watching all of this happen with small interest. I have become too Zen to be a writer in the way I used to be a writer.

All of this is useful to me as a teacher, however. I have learned that criticism is poison to a writer. Now, what am I going to do to help these students learn to write stories they can publish without hurting their feelings and making it impossible for them to write at all? I will teach them how to *kindly* edit their fellow students' work and maybe the lessons they learn by doing that will allow them to learn to look at their own work objectively. WRITING IS REWRITING I tell my students over and over again because *when I believed that* I published everything I wrote. Now I tell them that WRITING IS REWRITING but I no longer care to do it myself.

Perhaps I am telling myself stories to get myself ready for death. I will die in about thirty years if my genetic history is any indicator. Actually, I take such good care of myself that barring accidents I will probably live forty more years. So I don't think I'm getting ready to die. I just think I am tired of showing my imagination to the world and want to keep it to myself.

Or perhaps I am getting lazy. I don't think that's true because I have never been lazy in any way but you never can tell what Zen meditation may be making happen to my mind and psyche. Maybe I have actually learned to live in the present. I have been trying to learn to do that for many years. It may have happened while I wasn't watching.

I am happier than I have ever been in my life and more patient. HOORAY FOR EVERYTHING as a poet once wrote in the crazy 1970s when poets reigned supreme in the United States of America that I knew.

MARCH 2004

The Tar Baby

I'M IN SO DEEP I can't get out. I have started liking teaching more than I like writing. My students are doing well. One of my undergraduates won the departmental fiction award for a story he wrote in my workshop. My students have won the award *for three years in a row.* I'm terribly proud of them and proud of myself for inspiring them to *rewrite the stories until they were good.* This year's student, Kevin Brown, rewrote his story four times. We put it on the worksheet three times. He believed me when I told him that writing is rewriting and now he has his reward. His face was glowing as he ran into my office to tell me the news. He said it was the best thing that ever happened to him in his life.

Where in sitting all alone at my typewriter is there any emotion to compete with this? There isn't. And that is why people stop writing after they start teaching.

Teaching is fun! It's exciting and challenging and full of surprises. I have been teaching for four years now. My students work all over Fayetteville. If I go down on Dickson Street to get a smoothie one of my students makes it for me. If I have a flat tire in front of the Whole Foods Market a student is standing there to help me. If I go to Target to see the new clothes Isaac Mizrahi designed, I run into one of my graduate students and she helps me buy a seersucker skirt and later we go to my house and drink ginger tea and walk around the yard and look at the prayer flags I hung on my trees to bring luck to the students' writing.

Teaching has filled my life with wonderful, imaginative young people. My own grandchildren are far away from me. I talk to them on the phone and see them in the summer and at Christmas but I don't have them with me every day. My students are all around me. They enrich my life, they teach me things, they give me books to read and tell me about music I would never have known about. The chairman of our department is an aficionado of African music. He has a radio program on Monday nights of music from all the African countries. I would never have known this wonderful music if I hadn't met Robert Brinkmeyer. Now I am addicted to it and listen every Monday night.

My poor old writing has suffered. I write books still. I have written two or three of them in the last couple of years but I don't REWRITE THEM ANYMORE. I tell the students that writing is rewriting but I do not tell them that it is hard, arduous work. They can find that out for themselves and the ambitious, driven ones will find it out. Let them rewrite their stories and win awards. I'm through with all of that. I have a job I absolutely love, a paycheck every month, a retirement account, a rich and full life. Why should I spend my mornings rewriting my stories to make them into something the world will find valuable enough to print and read? I like them as they are. If I go back into boxes of my papers and find first drafts of things I have published, often I like the first drafts better than I like the finished PRODUCT.

I'm tired of turning my wild imagination into PRODUCT.

Here is what I'm doing with my life in the last year before I am seventy years old. Exercise, careful diet, devotion to beauty and order, devotion to my children and grandchildren, being here in good health and good spirits for when they need help or advice, enjoying the wonderful house I bought with money I made writing books, enjoying the spring rains and winter snows and flowers and trees and all the beauties of the earth and sky. I am meditating and doing yoga and reading Shakespeare with my friends on Sunday afternoon.

Last week I went on a news fast, an idea I got from Doctor Andrew Weil, who is my spiritual guru. After fourteen days of my fast, I put on my glasses while running on a treadmill at the gym. The first thing that flashed across the screen was a story about a man in

California who had shot all seven of his children in their faces with a gun and killed them all.

I took off my glasses. My news fast may last another month. Or forever. I already know who to vote for. I don't need commentators who have been corrupted by making hundreds of thousands of dollars a year to tell me what to think about the events of the world.

Teaching is a tar baby. I'm stuck and I love it. I don't even want to get away although I am always glad when a semester is over and I can go back to writing first drafts of novels and stories and putting them away in boxes to read when I am old. I probably won't get old. That may not be as inescapable as some people seem to think it is.

FEBRUARY 2004